Praise for *Made, Known, Loved*

"You've been asking God how you can minister effectively to LGBTQ+ youth, and now Ross Murray has written *Made, Known, Loved*. Funny how God works, isn't it?"
—Azariah Southworth, host, *Yass, Jesus!* podcast

"If you are looking for a book on youth ministry for LGBTQ youth, this book is well worth your time. But what Ross Murray does even more powerfully is to remind us that LGBTQ kids are so much more than their labels—that like all youth, they are figuring out who they are, what that means, and how they fit into the world. In *Made, Known, Loved*, he reminds us that LGBTQ youth need exactly the same things as the rest of the youth group: a place to be safe, a place to be loved, a place to be themselves, and a place to learn what it means to be adored by God."
—Kristen E. M. Kuempel, bishop, Northwest Intermountain Synod, ELCA

"*Made, Known, Loved* is a rare and wonderful book that will help save lives. There are books on LGBTQ people; there are books on Christian ministry; there are even books on youth ministry. But this is the first book I know of that addresses the important topic of Christian ministry to LGBTQ youth, who often feel rejected by their families, shut out from their churches, and abandoned by God. Ross Murray reminds the readers, whom I hope will be not only ministers but also young people and their families, that LGBTQ people are, as Psalm 139 says, 'wonderfully made.'"
—James Martin, SJ, Jesuit priest and author of *Building a Bridge*, about LGBTQ Catholics

"Ross Murray has a heart as big as the world. His clear and generous book provides strategies for making youth ministries more welcoming of LGBTQ people—but just as important, it's a meditation on the radical, transformational love of God. *Made, Known, Loved* will change lives, restore hope, and open hearts."
—Jennifer Finney Boylan, author of *She's Not There* and *Good Boy*

"*Made, Known, Loved* is the resource the church has been waiting for as we seek to do right by queer young people in our ministries and communities. Filled with personal stories, sound theology, practical tips, and a lot of love and hope, Ross Murray's book will guide and inspire your ministry with youth."

—Molly Beck Dean, director, ELCA Youth Gathering

"Ross Murray is a proven educator and advocate who leads essential work at the intersection of faith communities and LGBTQ people of faith. *Made, Known, Loved* is a critical resource at a critical time for Christian leaders who want to be allies but don't always know how. Murray's work to include LGBTQ youth is urgent. The compelling personal stories and expert guidance in his timely resource will not merely enlighten and inform adults but lead to programs and ministries that will raise the next generation of LGBTQ Christian advocates."

—Sarah Kate Ellis, president and CEO, GLAAD

"Ross Murray provides us with a book that is long overdue. In twenty-five pithy, thoughtful chapters, Murray addresses the questions youth ministers are asking about ministry with young people in the LGBTQ community—from the practical to the complex. Ross is a proven transformational leader, critical theologian, and compassionate minister. His experiences are broad and his insights deep. This book will become an important companion as you learn to queer your ministry and expand your congregation's proclamation of Christ's good news."

—Jeremy Myers, author of *Liberating Youth from Adolescence*; associate professor of theology and public leadership and executive director of the Christensen Center for Vocation, Augsburg University

"Practical, compassionate, and chock-full of the kind of wisdom that comes only from decades of walking alongside LGBTQ youth on their spiritual journey, *Made, Known, Loved* is a must-read for every youth pastor!"

—Jennifer Knapp, Grammy Award–nominated musician

"Too often a church is tempted to approach LGBTQ+ issues as something to be navigated—if the person can be categorized, then they can be understood. In *Made, Known, Loved*, Ross Murray leads us to a better understanding of churches' youth, queer and otherwise. He calls us to see each youth in their own dynamic personhood and context. My soul is refreshed by this and so much more in these pages."

—Noah Hepler, pastor, Lutheran Church of the Atonement, Philadelphia; participant in season 5, episode 1, of Netflix's *Queer Eye*

"Ross Murray offers all of us a gift in *Made, Known, Loved*: a reminder that we are 'fearfully and wonderfully made' (Psalm 139:14)—in the image of God. This is not a guide to accepting and loving LGBTQIA+ youth into the church. It is the reminder they are already the church—the body of Christ. Through Ross's own journey, he shows us how he came to know he was made, known, and loved by God and how we can claim that knowledge for ourselves and share it with others. Ross provides wisdom about how important safe spaces are for LGBTQIA+ persons and how much more the church can and should do to provide that sanctuary. Every youth ministry would benefit from this book's riches."

—Bishop Kevin L. Strickland, bishop, Southeastern Synod, ELCA

"*Made, Known, Loved* is a book I wish everyone would read as they seek to build more LGBTQIA+ spaces in their youth ministry. Ross Murray speaks important truths with grace and clarity for the reader, regardless of where they are on their journey. I already find myself using some of his just-in-time resources for my own life and ministry. For our church, which has too often separated faith and sexuality, this book is a must-read. I highly recommend it to anyone who takes gospel-centered inclusivity seriously."

—David Scherer, cofounder, Just Move: Anti-Racism through the Arts

"When church leaders seek to embody the love of God and welcome of Jesus in their youth ministry, improving the experience of LGBTQ+ youth is essential. With a compassion and wisdom formed by fifteen years of work with LGBTQ+ youth, Ross Murray offers a clear and comprehensive guide for the many questions that pastors, youth ministers, and parents might encounter. With instructive stories, contextual insight, and extensive resources, Murray provides a way forward through questions into action that will benefit not just a church's LGBTQ+ youth but the whole body of Christ."

—Emmy Kegler, author of *One Coin Found:*
How God's Love Stretches to the Margins

"*Made, Known, Loved* is the exact book needed for this exact time. Honestly and humbly, Ross Murray, guided by real-life experiences, deals with the questions that will help churches measure their inclusion of LGBTQ youth in their programs and also work with all youth. If the church is to be a no-judgment, safe, welcoming, and inclusive place, allowing people to learn and experience that God's love is for us all, then soak in the wisdom found here. This is the guidebook that will challenge and renew youth programs, camps, and the whole church."

—Lyle Griner, national director, Peer Ministry Leadership

"People who write endorsements for books do so primarily for two reasons—they believe in the importance of the topic, and they trust the voice of the author(s), often saying that this is an 'important' and 'needed' book. Well, guess what? Both reasons are true about this book—it couldn't be more important, timely, or needed. And indeed, I value and trust the voice and wisdom of this author and gifted leader, Ross Murray.

"Though Ross indicates in the introduction that this book is eminently practical, its deeper motivation is profoundly theological. That which is at the heart of God's being, revealed clearly and decisively in Jesus Christ, is Love—an immense, immeasurable, irrevocable, radically inclusive love for this whole creation and all of its peoples. Friends, this book is a gift and a call to church in all of its expressions to authenticate and seek to imitate in our lives and in our communities God's expansive and unconditional love for all people, particularly God's beloved LGBTQ+ young humans."

—Nathan C. P. Frambach, professor of pastoral theology, Wartburg Theological Seminary

MADE, KNOWN, LOVED

MADE, KNOWN, LOVED

DEVELOPING LGBTQ-INCLUSIVE YOUTH MINISTRY

ROSS MURRAY

FORTRESS PRESS

MINNEAPOLIS

This book is dedicated to LGBTQ youth who are still learning who God made them to be and how God is calling them in the world, as well as to the adults who are creating safe spaces to allow youth to do just that.

IN MEMORIAM

For Megan and Ray,
two beloved children of God whose calling to ministry included
The Naming Project.
We are forever shaped by your ministry of presence.

CONTENTS

ACKNOWLEDGMENTS

This book has been the culmination of seventeen years of ministry and the wisdom of hundreds of people who made it possible. Putting it into book form was a new and exciting challenge for me. I appreciate the people at 1517 Media for giving me the opportunity to share whatever wisdom I've picked up through this ministry, Beth Gaede for shepherding me through the process, and Ulrike Guthrie for editing my voice to be effective and powerful.

My deepest appreciation for all the adult leaders who have given their time and expertise to make The Naming Project work. Pastors Brad Froslee, Jay Wiesner, and I created The Naming Project out of nothing, using our creativity and energy to pull together the best practices we had at the time. I am so thankful to have had some of the best cofounders possible for this ministry. Special thanks to Greg Fedio and Logan Rimel, who picked up the mantle of leadership and took The Naming Project to the next level.

Thanks to my parents and sister for exemplifying the love and acceptance of God, allowing me to create a ministry that helps others discover God's love and acceptance for themselves. Love to my husband, Richard Garnett, for being patient, encouraging, and supportive throughout the work of The Naming Project. He has listened to my camp stories, overheard conference calls, edited web pages, consoled me in times of grief, and distracted me when I got into my head too much.

Pastors Megan Jane Jones and Ray McKechnie in particular shaped the ministry. Both passed away too soon, but their presence and ministry shaped what The Naming Project is.

To the hundreds of youth who have been a part of The Naming Project since its foundation: your participation, storytelling, singing, prayers, and questions have made The Naming Project the ministry it is today.

Praise and thanks to God, who created us, knows us intimately, and loves us just as we are.

INTRODUCTION

"What do lesbians do? I mean, sexually?" the woman asked me. Even though I'd been working for months with a couple of friends to create a safe space for LGBTQ youth to talk about faith, I was not prepared for her question.[1] Lesbian sexual practices weren't something I'd spent much time or energy thinking about as a twentysomething gay man.

The questioner and I were at a crowded reception at a youth ministry conference. She'd been in the workshop I'd just finished teaching about the creation of The Naming Project, a ministry to meet the spiritual needs of LGBTQ youth.

"I'm mentoring a girl at my church," she continued, "and she's starting to share a little bit with me about her self-discovery. It's great that she feels that she can trust me, but she's asking me questions that I don't know how to answer. I was hoping you could educate me."

I also looked around, suddenly aware that if overheard, my honest answer might cause some consternation at this youth ministry conference.

In my discomfort, I almost cracked a joke. But I realized that I was standing before a very well-intentioned, straight, cisgender woman who wanted to be a good adult mentor for a young child of God who had some real questions about what she was "supposed" to do or what was "OK" to do. She'd just met me, but this woman had worked up the courage to ask me a serious question. She deserved a serious response.

Her question took me back to an earlier time before we had ever conceived of The Naming Project. In a panel discussion about the faith needs of LGBTQ youth, a youth minister in the audience shared that she felt completely unprepared for what to do if one of the youth at her church came out to her: "I want to be supportive and helpful, but I don't know what the right thing to do is. I'm scared I'll say nothing, or at least nothing helpful, and then the youth will think I'm not supportive, and I am, but I don't know how to be."

This youth minister had been a friend of mine for years. She had been supportive of my coming out and my identity as an openly gay Christian. I (and others in her life) had taught her something about being an LGBTQ person who keeps his faith, and now youth were looking to her to teach them about the relationship between Christianity and LGBTQ people.

Her question made me aware of how much the church's erasure, rejection, and lack of understanding were going to hurt youth. Both of these women were identifying where the church has historically fallen short even without always being explicitly anti-LGBTQ. Such questions are learning opportunities for the church—if the institution is willing to do that work.

There are many people in the church who intend to listen, learn, and work, but the everyday demands of ministry often negate those good intentions. Rather than recognize LGBTQ youth as unique creatures with unique needs, such persons erase sexual orientation or gender identity, burying it in a culture of assumed heterosexuality and cisgender identity (the notion that one's internal sense of gender matches the way they are perceived externally). Or if well-meaning church folks do validate LGBTQ sexual orientations and gender identities, those sexual orientations and gender identities are considered something separate from the person's growing faith identity.

Unintentionally or not, erasing LGBTQ youth or treating their sexual orientation or gender identity as completely separate from their faith leaves LGBTQ youth with no community in which to integrate their faith, sexual orientation, and gender identity. In a perfect world, every community is one in which all aspects of identity can be explored. But historically, we pick apart a person's identity, treating its various aspects as separate and occasionally competing.

Fielding questions *about* LGBTQ youth and faith has become pretty routine in the time I've been running The Naming Project. Over the past fifteen years, my fellow creators and leaders of this youth ministry have been asked many times "how best to" accommodate LGBTQ youth, decide on sleeping arrangements, use language and terminology, find trusted local resources, and so on.

Most of the questions are from straight, cisgender pastors and youth ministers, like the two women who lobbed questions at me on different occasions. Such persons are loving and want to be affirming, but they haven't been involved in the LGBTQ community and may be unfamiliar with the language and terminology that LGBTQ youth use to describe themselves. They are often scared that even the wording of their question might offend me. And some feel shame for not already knowing the answer.

Most of the time, pastors and youth ministers fall into one of two categories: either they want answers to quick, logistical questions—such as about updating their existing church policies or figuring out sleeping arrangements on a trip—or they describe elaborate scenarios and end with "Any advice on what we should do?"

Common examples of such questions include the following:

- Can you share with us thoughts or resources you have for a youth ministry geared to LGBTQ or confused/transitioning teens and youth to come and worship free of judgment or fear of someone trying to "fix" them? We feel that it is a need that has not been met in our state and that it is a large one.
- Our church is looking for ways to reach out to LGBTQ high school students, particularly those who fear that their churches or families will never accept them for who they are. We know there's a great need, but we don't have a clear idea to what kind of programming youth will respond best. How did you initially draw up your program, and how has it evolved? Do you carry most of the leadership, or do you bring in resource people from farther away? Do you have any background material on your programs that you could send us?

- What kind of praise have you received from parents and congregations? Likewise, what kind of backlash?
- When starting your ministry, what resources did you already have, and what did you need to get in order to get the program off the ground?
- How do you handle sleeping accommodations during camps and trips with LGBTQ youth?
- A high school teacher in our congregation asked me if I had any suggestions for how she might help a student whose father is a less-affirming pastor. The student told her teacher that she thinks her family would disown her if she came out as bisexual. She lives in a very small town, so any local/regional resources might be difficult for her to access in a way that feels safe for her. I am wondering if you could recommend particular online support groups / safe spaces for this student.[2]

As the first and largest LGBTQ Christian youth ministry program in the United States, The Naming Project has had to think through these questions. People write to us because they believe they can learn from our experience.

The Naming Project started with a question and a plea for help from a woman I considered a mentor. My first job out of college was providing logistical and planning support for a youth and family ministry institute. One of the executives at the organization was a woman named Marilyn Sharpe. She was a confirmation and parenting guru, having led both a youth confirmation group and a support group for mothers at a huge area church for decades. She had an adult lesbian daughter who had already opened Marilyn's eyes to the realities of LGBTQ people. Marilyn was vocally supportive, making sure I knew that I was welcome and supported in my work at the youth and family ministry institute.

One day, Marilyn came by my desk with a request for help. A friend at her church, the wife of one of the pastors, had approached Marilyn with a question about a fifteen-year-old son who had come out to his parents. The parents were accepting, and they wanted to find him a community where he could be around peers who were also growing up and coming out.

The family tried attending a local LGBTQ youth center, but it wasn't a good cultural fit for the son. The youth at the center had been on the receiving end of discrimination and even abuse. Some were forbidden to speak about being LGBTQ at home. Some had been kicked out of their homes. They were couch surfing or, in some cases, living on the street, doing whatever they needed to do to survive. Many saw the church as the source of their troubles, and they had no interest in engaging with any kind of church ministry, even if it was affirming.

Sometimes such youth and families seeking local resources will find a caring environment in which the youth can explore their sexual identity in a caring group of peers and guiding adults. Most often, these environments are secular. Their leaders are not equipped to explore spirituality issues. In many cases, the adults leading the programs have their own baggage around faith and their involvement with faith communities. They feel that exploring spirituality is a role for individual faith communities, not the group they lead.

The boy in question was a suburban teenager with two parents who continued to accept, love, and support him. In so many ways, he was blessed and privileged. The family was shocked to discover that other youth often aren't accepted and the extremes to which they have to go to survive. The reality is that 40 percent of the homeless youth population identifies as LGBTQ despite being less than 10 percent of the total youth population.[3] Nearly 90 percent of homeless LGBTQ youth are homeless specifically because they are LGBTQ.

The family didn't realize how much they were bucking a trend by trying to support their son. Their eyes had been opened to the reality of many LGBTQ youth, but they were no closer to finding their son peers who would help and support him in coming out and living out his values as a Christian.

They tried LGBTQ-focused and LGBTQ-friendly churches, but the congregations seemed to be filled with adults. If there were youth, they were the children of LGBTQ parents and often were much younger and straight. There were no out youth in any of the congregations. The other churches were either hostile about or silent on LGBTQ issues.

The responsibility for learning must fall on the church and its leaders. If the church isn't willing to learn, it abandons youth to try to learn more about their sexual orientation or gender identity on their own, with little control of the quality of information they are receiving. Where youth go for information and guidance can often lead them on a dangerous path of half-truths, misinformation, and even exploitation. If they search online to explore their sexual orientation or gender identity, LGBTQ youth will often land with harmful people and in unsafe situations.

In short, if churches are too squeamish to talk about sexuality with youth, youth go elsewhere to develop their identities as sexual beings. Since LGBTQ youth are not a part of mainstream culture, they have to find special environments to explore their sexuality. Those environments either are often destructive or at least lack the spiritual foundation of churches. In the least-bad scenario, these youth develop spiritual and sexual identities that are miles apart. In the worst situations, LGBTQ youth deny one or another part of their identity.

One day, the aforementioned concerned mother came home from work to find a forty-year-old man waiting on her doorstep. In looking for a community that could support and inform him as a gay boy, the son had found online chat rooms and community groups. He connected and conversed with an older man. Through the chat, the youth had provided enough information for the man to find his house, and the man was paying him a visit.

The mother was rightly alarmed at a stranger being at her house to visit her son. It prompted her to reach out more urgently to everyone she knew, asking for church-based LGBTQ youth groups. The question had come to Marilyn, and Marilyn was now presenting it to me. Marilyn also brought the same story and question to my friend and colleague Jay Wiesner. We told her we didn't know of any such groups but that we'd look into it.

There are organizations within every Christian denomination actively working to help integrate faith identity, sexual orientation, and gender identity. Originally created in the 1970s to provide safe places for LGBTQ people to worship without the fear of being outed and losing their church, family, or jobs, these organizations evolved into advocates for LGBTQ-inclusive policies in denominations. ReconcilingWorks,[4] More Light Presbyterians, Dignity

(Catholic), Integrity (Episcopalian), and countless other LGBTQ denominational groups have been working for a number of years to address faith and sexuality in a substantial and holistic way.[5]

When Jay and I looked closer, we found that many of these advocacy groups did not include youth as a part of their mission. For example, when I was first getting involved with the Lutheran group ReconcilingWorks in the early 2000s, the organization had a policy of not engaging with anyone under eighteen years old. The perception that LGBTQ folks are predatory or dangerous to young people had kept these faithful LGBTQ adults from mentoring or sharing their faith with younger LGBTQ Christians. These faithful adults did not want to be accused of "recruiting" youth into a "homosexual lifestyle." They knew that even an unfounded accusation would ruin the reputation of their group.

The organizations for LGBTQ youth didn't address religion. The religious youth groups didn't address LGBTQ issues. And the religious organizations that addressed both LGBTQ issues and religion excluded youth. It was as if of the three—religion, youth, and LGBTQ issues—any group could only address two at once.

The Open and Affirming Coalition of the United Church of Christ was an exception. The organization employed a staff member to deal with youth and young adult issues and had compiled a bibliography of resources for pastors, youth, and families. A couple of people mentioned rumors of a Jewish LGBTQ youth program, but we never did manage to find evidence of its existence. These organizations and their programs were designed by and for baby boomers (the first generation to be bold enough to come out at all). They often don't connect with the current situation of youth who live in a very different context.

Jay and I sat down with Marilyn in our office and reported our findings—or lack of findings. After sharing that we couldn't find any active LGBTQ youth groups for this family, we looked at each other and said, "Well, we'll need to create something."

Marilyn told me later she nearly burst into tears at our spontaneous decision to create an LGBTQ youth ministry that hadn't existed until that point.

But now that we had said it, we had to figure out how to do it! And that came with its own set of challenges. Empowered by Marilyn's questions and her support for this new ministry, we set about developing what an LGBTQ youth ministry might look like.

All that history—the suburban boy and his family, the well-meaning but ignorant youth ministers, the reality that churches were not equipped to deal with LGBTQ organizations while many LGBTQ organizations were unequipped to deal with issues of religion or faith—led to the creation of The Naming Project, an LGBTQ youth ministry, which led to the questions that came pouring in.

This book is an attempt to address many of those questions as well as the assumptions behind those questions. For pastors and youth ministers, this book may present as a "how-to" manual. How to what? That depends on you and your situation. You could read this and decide that you want to create your own LGBTQ youth ministry. You can look at the decisions we made and the policies we set and create something that is an even more effective ministry than what we did. You could be reading this and wondering how to make your church's youth ministry more inclusive of LGBTQ young people. In that case, we hope you find some of our best practices and our rationale for those practices to be helpful. Perhaps you want some games or arts and crafts ideas to re-create with your church. You'll find a few in here as well. How you use this book is up to you.

This book is a balancing act for me to write, and it needs to be a balancing act for you, the reader. If you bought this book to read it like an instruction manual, looking for step-by-step instructions for how to treat LGBTQ youth who interact with your youth ministry, you will be disappointed. For if I give you a set of rules and guidelines to follow based on what works for us, you'll likely find they won't work for you and your context. Every setting is different. Every youth identifies in their particular way, has different comfort levels, and expresses themselves in a different way.

I don't have all the answers about LGBTQ youth ministry. The only person who fully knows the hearts and minds of LGBTQ youth is the God who created them, knows them, and loves them just as they are. We figured out a lot about such youth ministry through a painful process of trial and error. We made mistakes, we changed our minds, we learned more as we went along, and still today, we make mistakes. We work in a specific setting with specific (and changing) facilities.

In other ways, this book is a memoir. It's a way for you to get a glimpse into our hearts and minds during the processes of creating an LGBTQ youth ministry at a time when none existed. There may still be something you can learn from our experiences, our successes, and our failures. You can avoid the mistakes we made and the prejudices we had to unlearn. In your own particular way, you can replicate what worked for us. You can judge us, be inspired by us, or just find our path interesting. Take what works for you and leave the rest of it.

Another disclaimer: this book is about Christian ministry, even though youth programs of other faiths may find aspects of what we did helpful. I am a Lutheran who speaks and moves in Lutheran theology, reflecting my Christian experience. There is a need to create similar organizations for the youth of many faiths (and no faith at all). But those books should be written by people who identify with their particular faith just as I identify with the Lutheran branch of Christianity.

With those disclaimers established, I invite you into this unique, frustrating, campy, and very queer form of youth ministry. Be prepared to have your heart both nurtured and challenged—not by this book but by the experiences you will have with LGBTQ youth who are seeking answers about themselves and their relationship with God.

CHAPTER

1

WHAT QUESTIONS SHOULD I BE ASKING ABOUT LGBTQ YOUTH MINISTRY?

"How do you do sleeping arrangements?"

This is the question first and most frequently asked of us at The Naming Project. It's not a bad question. But fundamentally that question, and others like it, considers LGBTQ youth as a logistical problem to be solved.

Logistical questions cannot be answered out of context. The way The Naming Project organized sleeping arrangements at our camp has evolved over time and in response to a changing context. I'll tell that story later. First, I want to address the mindset we Christian leaders need to have when we are considering how to make our congregations and ministries inclusive for LGBTQ youth.

Instead of focusing on logistics, start with your congregation's or group's identity and values. Ask yourself, What are the values your congregation or your camp has for the youth who participate in your ministry? What are your values around the welcoming and acceptance of LGBTQ youth? How does the theology of *imago Dei*, grace through faith, and vocation determine your ministry with LGBTQ youth? If you haven't thought about how an LGBTQ youth might experience and understand theological concepts before, then it's time to start thinking about it now.

When we were first establishing The Naming Project, we talked extensively with youth experts, social workers, and those who worked in the LGBTQ space to see if this idea could fly. One social worker liked our idea but challenged us to define our identity further. "Is this a Lutheran program, a Christian program, a religion program, or a spirituality program?" she asked. "How you define what sort of group this is will change who is interested, what you offer, and for what you need to be prepared."

Her question forced us to pause. It wasn't a question we had considered. Having grown up in the Lutheran church, I probably had a rather myopic vision of the world. I assumed that the whole world looked like the Lutheran church in which I grew up. Her question pushed me to broaden my vision.

Jay and I discussed it. As Christian ministers, we knew we weren't going to be helpful to youth who had questions about the theology, values, and world-views of non-Christian faiths, youth such as the Muslim Somali kids in the Minneapolis neighborhood where Jay's church was located. We imagined that an LGBTQ Muslim youth might hear about our program and approach us for help. We had a hard time imagining how we could competently support them, since we knew relatively little about Muslim faith or Somali family dynamics. We wanted to be able to point the youth toward affirming congregations, but at the time, we didn't know non-Christian affirming religious groups.

There weren't enough LGBTQ Lutheran youth to warrant a program just for them, even in the Lutheran-dense Twin Cities, so we had to think of a program for a wider range of youth. Eventually, we decided to offer a Christian LGBTQ youth ministry for any youth. We could be supportive of youth who weren't Christian, but we would be running the program with Christian principles and values that would guide how we led. That would allow us to lead and teach from a place of integrity while also being open to listening to the lived experiences the youth brought to us.

Your particular values will likewise inform your actions. Youth ministries that see LGBTQ youth as damaged or dangerous will treat them as such. They will enact policies that police rather than protect LGBTQ youth. When encountering a logistical problem—especially when it involves people, especially young people, *especially* LGBTQ youth and other marginalized groups—it's often helpful to step back to examine your values. Values transcend logistics, and values are played out logistically in different contexts.

By now you'll have realized that I'm not going to spend any time or energy convincing you that sexual orientation and gender identity are a part of God's creation, including LGBTQ sexual orientations or gender identities. I'm not going to rehash the biblical arguments, because others have done that better than I could. Take a look at Appendix A to see a fuller resource list.

Instead, I'm assuming that you recognize that there are LGBTQ youth in your congregation, and you intend them to be able to be open about their full, authentic selves at church. If you don't share this assumption, then this book may not be helpful to you. If your values include maintaining a binary view of the world, of keeping people in a specific role, or that LGBTQ people are flawed and cannot participate fully in the church and society, then flip to some of the resources in Appendix A that make the case that LGBTQ people were created by God, were endowed with inherent dignity and worth, and are called to full participation in the church and the world.

When we were first establishing The Naming Project, our values informed our actions. But we also intentionally wrote a mission statement and a goal statement that laid out those values and how we would live them out. This was the result:

> The mission of The Naming Project is to create places of safety for youth of all sexual orientations and gender identities where faith is shared and healthy life-giving community is modeled.
>
> The goal of The Naming Project is to provide a safe and sacred space where youth of all sexual orientations and gender identities are named and claimed by a loving God; can explore and share faith; experience healthy and life-giving community; reach out to others; and advocate for systemic change in church and society.[1]

The mission statement and the goal statement highlight a few of our values:

- *LGBTQ youth are created and known by a loving God*, who hasn't made a mistake in creation—a God whose creation includes a diverse range of sexual orientations and gender identities.
- *Youth can be who they are.* We assumed that our youth were living in a world that wasn't letting them be fully and authentically themselves. In order to get by, they were suppressing their sexual orientation or gender identity. Some were "performing" exceptionally well so that no one viewed them as "deficient" in any way. They felt like they had to be the "right" kind of Christian.
- *Youth will not be judged.* We want to ensure that youth can enter our space with all their doubts and uncertainties. We want them to be able to be honest about figuring out who they are, how they identify, and what language they use to talk about themselves. We won't pressure them into being our version of either LGBTQ or Christian. We want to make sure that youth are making wise choices and keeping themselves safe, without judging or shaming them for whatever they have done. We want to be able to listen and provide guidance from a place that comes from support, not judgment.
- *Youth will be safe.* Safety is multifaceted. Just as we don't want youth to slip and break a leg while they are in our program, so too we don't want them to be harassed or sexualized by adults or other youth. We don't want them to be belittled for who they are and what they believe. If we cannot assure their safety, then we should not be operating a youth ministry, much less an LGBTQ youth ministry.
- *LGBTQ youth respond to the gospel.* We don't shy away from sharing the gospel with LGBTQ youth, even as we welcome them from wherever they are. We invite exploration of Scripture, connecting the stories of Scripture to their daily lives.

Marcus,[2] one of our early participants, put it this way: "I want to come here and be as gay as I want and have as many doubts as I can have, and I won't be hit on or made to feel like I'm not good enough."

These guidelines were simple to set, but keeping them takes intentionality and work. Safety doesn't just happen, no matter how much we want it to or how much we talk about it. We have to pray for the best and be fully prepared for the worst.

With those values articulated, we could then look at each context as it came up to make decisions about what would work in whatever space we were doing ministry. Along the way, that did also include sleeping arrangements. But that comes later.

CHAPTER

2

WHAT IF I ENCOUNTER RESISTANCE ESTABLISHING AN LGBTQ YOUTH MINISTRY?

You've decided that your youth ministry is going to be intentionally welcoming to LGBTQ youth. Your values include the beliefs that God created LGBTQ youth in love and that they, like all youth, need an opportunity to grow in faith in a safe and caring environment.

Perhaps you are establishing this youth ministry out of a personal conviction. Perhaps you are doing it because you are a parent of an LGBTQ youth and want a safe and caring place for your own child. Perhaps, like me, you are doing this because you are an LGBTQ adult, and you want to create the safe and caring group in your church that you didn't have as a youth.

No matter how personally convicted you are to take steps to be more welcoming and inclusive to LGBTQ youth, because you are working within a wider context, you will encounter resistance. It is possible that your congregation isn't as welcoming to LGBTQ people as you want your youth group to be. Your pastor may not be as accepting as you are. You may have members of your congregation who oppose the idea of including LGBTQ youth or want to put restrictions on youths' participation. Or you may be in a community that is much less accepting than your congregation is. You can still take steps to make your youth group a welcoming place, but if you encounter resistance, your work will be more difficult. Be prepared.

In a perfect world, the congregation would be just as much of a welcoming place as the youth ministry. Some congregations have designated themselves as open to LGBTQ people. Programs like Reconciling in Christ in the Lutheran Church or Open and Affirming in the United Church of Christ maintain rosters of congregations who have made an explicit statement of welcome that includes LGBTQ people.[1] These designations are usually accomplished through a congregation-wide process to understand what it means to include LGBTQ people and to ensure that the congregation wholly supports it.[2] The statements rarely include mention of youth specifically, but an overall declaration of welcome for the congregation will have a strong impact on the youth ministry of the congregation.

It's worthwhile to work toward an LGBTQ welcoming statement for the entire congregation, but it can be a years-long process, and you might become frustrated at the slow pace. You just want your youth ministry to be a hospitable place. How do you achieve that?

First, make youth aware that you are a safe conversation partner even if you believe no one else in the congregation is. If a youth is looking for an adult to come out to, they will be looking for hints that you are a safe person. A door sign or sticker, especially with a rainbow, is an effective way to visually communicate where LGBTQ-friendly places are. The rainbow can be as prominent or as subtle as needed.

The practice of dropping a subtle signal like this isn't new. It's what the early Christians did to identify one another. The now common *ichthys*, or "Jesus fish" symbol, was used starting in the second century, when Christians were still being persecuted by the Roman Empire. The symbol was a way of hiding in plain sight. Someone not familiar with the symbol would miss it, while Christians would recognize the symbol as an indication that the location or the people were fellow Christians and presumably safe.

The rainbow flag has served a similar purpose for LGBTQ people. Especially in hostile environments, the rainbow flag has been placed on the doors of businesses, homes, and even churches to communicate "This is a safe place." Symbols like this have become important, especially in states that have passed laws allowing businesses to refuse service to LGBTQ people. The rainbow sticker communicates that LGBTQ people will not be turned away, saving them significant shame and humiliation.

The same principle can apply to your desk or door inside of the church. Even if the rest of the congregation is ambivalent or hostile to LGBTQ people, you can use a subtle rainbow sticker to indicate that you are a safe person.

If you want to demonstrate a deeper awareness of the nuances of each of the communities under the broader LGBTQ umbrella, research the other flags associated with it. Each subcommunity has its own flag with its own color scheme. The transgender flag is pink, white, and pastel blue. The bisexual flag is a much bolder pink, blue, and purple. The list goes on and on. While the rainbow flag can communicate a pretty generic welcome, these more nuanced flags and color schemes demonstrate your awareness of youth who are transgender, bisexual, and so on. If you want to signify awareness and acceptance for specific communities, place these flags and color schemes at your desk space. People who aren't aware of the nuances of the LGBTQ community may not recognize these color schemes, but any youth who identifies with one of these communities will notice and will feel even more seen and welcomed by you.

Of course, if you display a symbol that signifies that you are a safe and welcoming person, your words and actions need to back that up. Proactively bring up the reality of LGBTQ people and the issues they face. It may be in reflecting on the week's news, or referencing an inclusive television show, or mentioning well-known LGBTQ people. You don't need to talk at length or make any protracted sermons about them. If you have to be subtle, no explanation or justification is needed. It is enough to acknowledge that you are aware of the reality of LGBTQ people in your life, in your community, and in our world.

You can reinforce your values about what sort of youth group you will be. Speak of safety and acceptance as your group's core values. Underline God's unconditional love and remind youth that you are trying to imitate that unconditional love. When proactively stated before the full youth group, these values will let any youth who is questioning their own identity know that you are a safe person. You are walking the walk.

If a youth does trust you enough to confide in you about their self-discovery and you know that you are in a less-than-accepting environment, you have a careful balancing act to negotiate. You want to support the youth and also keep them safe. This requires being honest with them about how the rest of the congregation feels even while assuring them of your own ongoing support. Remain professional; do not gossip, but be honest with the youth about what challenges they might encounter and where they can find allies within the congregation and community.

One of the biggest challenges will be if your church's pastor is anti-LGBTQ. If you are a professional youth minister, this person is likely your boss, who has much more direct control over your actions. Even if your pastor is not your boss, they wield significant influence over the congregation.

Other times, the resistance will come from other parishioners or even from outside the congregation. People may notice your rainbow sticker. They may see out and proud LGBTQ youth participating in the youth group, which will trigger their own anxieties. They may speak to you directly about their opposition to or fears about an inclusive youth ministry. They may speak to the pastor or to other members. They may try to sabotage your work by spreading gossip and misinformation about you and your ministry. The mere presence of openly LGBTQ people—including a drag queen story hour at local libraries and teachers being honest about their lives and their relationships—has elicited accusations of "sexualizing" the youth. Expect it and be prepared for it.

When we were forming The Naming Project, we were well aware that a youth ministry started by gay men would be open to suspicion. Around the time we began promoting The Naming Project, an anti-LGBTQ activist organization circulated an anonymous newsletter that used words like *report* and *expose* to talk about LGBTQ-affirming people and ministries. The newsletter described The Naming Project as "a 'ministry' called The Naming Project, which connects gay men with Twin Cities youth who have same sex attractions—offering these kids 'support.'"[3] That sentence was both laughable and a threat to us and our program. It became another reason we needed to have a solid risk-management plan in place. We knew we couldn't prevent someone from making such an accusation. But we could make sure our program was safe and secure for the youth who participated in it.

This is why starting with values is the most important part of developing an LGBTQ-inclusive youth ministry. We are being inclusive not just for the sake of inclusion but for the sake of the gospel. For The Naming Project, our mission statement speaks to the values we have: "The mission of The Naming Project is to create places of safety for youth of all sexual orientations and gender identities where faith is shared and healthy life-giving community is modeled." Creating a safe place, sharing faith, and nourishing a life-giving community aren't strictly LGBTQ values but values that would exemplify any good youth ministry.

You will not be able to eliminate resistance completely, nor will you be able to shield LGBTQ youth from discrimination and prejudice. Assessing where resistance might come from and being prepared will help you determine the best course of action. Will the resistance come from the pastoral leadership? Will it come from a single person or a section of membership? Will it come from the wider community? Dealing with each of these requires a different tactic and approach, and you'll want to think ahead of time about how you want to deal with each of those very real possibilities.

And occasionally, you will be blindsided. After a few years of running our summer camp, a documentary about our youth ministry came out, titled *Camp Out*. When the DVD was made available, Brenda Olson, the director of Bay Lake Camp, where The Naming Project holds our summer camp, called me.[4]

"Ross, someone has been putting flyers for *Camp Out* under the windshield wipers of all the cars around the lake. They look . . . odd."

She sent me a copy, and they *were* odd. They looked like an advertisement for purchasing the DVD but described the camp and the film in ways that I would never have done:

Filmed entirely at Bay Lake Camp, on beautiful Bay Lake, Deerwood, MN!

Discover the real-life adventures of ten Midwestern teenagers as they attend Bible Camp on an island in Northern Minnesota. They come from ten very different backgrounds, but these brave teens leave sharing a singular strong common bond. This heart-felt story uncovers many of the emotions and anxieties facing today's youth and how the young teenagers were able to overcome their fears to find self-confidence and learn life-skills that will shape their lives and impact their families forever. Sure to inspire and encourage your family!

Just in time for Christmas! Stocking stuffers. Grandkids. Great team/group gifts. Youth sports teams. Boy Scouts/Girl Scouts. Church Youth Library.

And finally, the flyer included directions for how to order a DVD. The form was directed at us, at The Naming Project, and the price was set for five dollars higher than the film was available for on Amazon.

Nowhere in the description did the flyer mention that The Naming Project was an LGBTQ camp. Instead, it seemed to want people to purchase a video and then be horrified to discover an LGBTQ youth church camp in their backyard. It was clear that someone was passive-aggressively trying to foment anger at our camp's existence and ensure that we lose money.

We discussed it among our leadership and advisory board. We decided that few people were likely to order a DVD. And then we waited to see if any orders came in. Three did.

We purchased three DVDs from Amazon and mailed them out. We also enclosed a brochure about The Naming Project along with a letter that described openly and honestly what The Naming Project is. We also explained that we did not place the flyers and that we didn't know who was telling them to order from us at a loss. However, we were willing to honor the fact that they were interested in *Camp Out* in good faith.

Of the three buyers, one wrote us back. She said, "I bought this DVD, thinking it would be a good gift for my grandchildren, but it is not what I expected. This film is not appropriate for young children. I am requesting a refund."

After I vented my personal frustrations to Jay and Brad, we sent her a check for the money she had sent us. We also enclosed a letter to remind her that we did not advertise the *Camp Out* DVD, nor did we think it was the right film for young children.

The opposition you encounter might be as indirect as someone trying to undermine your ministry with misinformation, such as what happened to us. Or you may have more direct confrontation. But spend time brainstorming where and how your opposition will manifest itself and prepare yourself for possible graceful responses.

At the very least, if you can be a single welcoming and accepting person within a hostile environment, that will be lifesaving for a youth who needs it. If you are able to band together with other allies, you will be stronger. If you have the support of your pastor and the congregation, then your ministry can be even more innovative. Stand firm guided by your values, and you will be able to stand firm in the face of resistance to your ministry on behalf of LGBTQ youth.

CHAPTER

3

SHOULD I SET UP A PROGRAM EXCLUSIVELY FOR LGBTQ YOUTH? OR JUST PRACTICE INCLUSIVITY?

"Is it OK to invite a straight friend to come with me?"

This question was posed by one of our campers. She was on the verge of registration, but she was nervous about going to our camp for the first time with other youth she didn't know. She said that having a trusted friend with her would make her feel more comfortable.

Of course, she could invite her friend, we responded. We wanted The Naming Project to be a space that welcomed youth of all sexual orientations and gender identities even though we were an LGBTQ-specific youth ministry.

Near the end of the week, we were sharing around a circle. The straight friend said to the group, "I've never been in a space where I'm the minority as a straight person. You are all very nice and welcoming, but it feels really weird not to be able to relate to your thoughts and feelings."

The "weirdness" that the straight friend was feeling is what LGBTQ youth feel in nearly every setting they encounter. They know spaces were not designed with them in mind. They are keenly aware that their comfort, wants, and needs are secondary. No matter how welcoming they are, most spaces are heteronormative, meaning they carry the assumptions that all boys are the same, all girls are the same, and boys will form romantic or sexual feelings for girls and vice versa.

Heteronormativity pervades our culture. Movies and television shows rarely depict LGBTQ people, and when they do, they are often one dimensional and exist in support of a (straight and cisgender) leading character. Advertisements that feature romance or weddings are centered on straight couples, and when LGBTQ inclusion is depicted, backlash ensues from anti-LGBTQ organizations like One Million Moms.[1]

We engineered The Naming Project to be the reverse of heteronormativity. While we are open to allied youth attending our programs and our camp, the purpose of our ministry is centered on the lives and experiences of LGBTQ youth. The Naming Project is a "set-apart space" designed to provide respite from the heteronormative assumptions of the world. In order to be able to explore their identities, we believe that LGBTQ youth need to be freed from the expectations and pressures of a society dominated by straight and cisgender people.

I'm not saying that LGBTQ youth should exist only in dedicated LGBTQ spaces. Instead, I'm talking about the need for a retreat that helps LGBTQ youth center themselves and get some clarity about themselves and their relationship with God and the rest of the world. Sometimes, hostile and conflicting messages directed at LGBTQ youth, combined with the anxiety-causing navigation of the world, can cloud someone's perception of themselves. Enjoying some time surrounded by young people who share the same identity and experience can help bring clarity to one's own self-understanding.

Other times, LGBTQ youth benefit from being in a mixed environment with non-LGBTQ youth where they can listen to others and express their feelings. They can interact with others who aren't like them. They need both kinds of situations.

Most people reading this book will want to learn about how to make their existing youth ministry a welcoming space to youth who are LGBTQ and are not planning to start a whole new program geared specifically toward LGBTQ youth. However, we have been contacted a few times by pastors and youth ministers who have attempted to start an LGBTQ space such as The Naming Project.

Creating an LGBTQ-specific youth ministry can take many forms. The Naming Project started off with a weekly meeting in a church basement on Sunday afternoons. Local Twin Cities youth were invited to drop by for a couple of hours to be in fellowship with other LGBTQ youth and adults. Currently, our summer camp attracts youth from all over the country who travel so that they can spend a week on an island away from the rest of the world among a safe and faithful community. I've spoken with churches that have had weekly or monthly meetings. Others have occasional events, drag shows, talent shows, special worship services, and so on.

Admittedly, I am a programming person. I think of how to put together a program that can reach people. So when I first envisioned The Naming Project, I dreamed big. My original vision for The Naming Project was to create a drop-in center, one that provided open space for young people to hang out, participate in programs, and possibly share a meal. We would have throngs of youth with an army of screened and trained adult volunteers. Some adults were mixing and mingling, some were leading the program, and others were serving the meal.

To see how my vision lined up with the reality of what LGBTQ youth of the Twin Cities needed, we set out to talk to youth experts, social workers, and those who worked in the LGBTQ space. Did they think this idea would fly? We spent time assessing the need for an LGBTQ youth group focused on religion. We distributed surveys to LGBTQ-serving youth organizations in the Twin Cities area.

Of the youth who responded, most were already in some form of an LGBTQ organization, and about half of them were interested in an LGBTQ group focused on spirituality, but it depended on the context. One added a comment that general spirituality was fine but that they were not interested in Christianity. Hardly any of them attended religious services, but one expressed a desire to attend church. When we asked about what sort of activities they wanted to see, the responses were pretty evenly mixed among discussion, games, spirituality, leadership development, and movies, with Bible study trailing far behind in their responses.

The additional comments let us know there was passive interest but not fervent excitement:

"Sounds like a good idea. Many gay people have trouble with Christianity, including myself, so I think this would be helpful."

"I think it is great you are having this group. However, I am already pretty comfortable with my sexual orientation and spirituality, so I'm not interested."

"I am not interested if it is a religious gathering, but if it is just activities and such, it would be cool."

Jay reached out to a Safe Schools organizer in the Twin Cities, telling her about our vision for a faith-based LGBTQ youth group and asking for her feedback. She listened carefully but responded that her youth didn't really care much about religion at all.

"I don't see any use for a program that focuses on religion," she said. Disappointed, Jay thanked her for her time. About two weeks later, she called Jay to say, "I don't know what happened, but after we talked, my kids keep saying, 'My church says that God hates LGBTQ people!' and 'The Bible has been used against us for so long. What does it really say?' Would you come and talk to our youth about God and religion and stuff?"

Jay was more than happy to oblige.

We finally decided that we had spent enough time doing research and planning and that we'd simply launch something. The format we settled on was a two-hour drop-in meeting time at Jay's church, Bethany Lutheran, on Sunday afternoons. We let our contacts and friends know that we were planning to start in April. Jay let the youth of his congregation know. Some responded that they would not be able to attend on our first date but expressed a general interest. The plan was that we'd meet in Jay's office in the church. It was a small space, but we would make it work.

We put a sign and doorbell on the doors outside the church, and then we waited.

After several minutes of wondering if we'd get any attendees, the doorbell rang. We rushed to greet our first participant. At the door, we found Marcus, a sixteen-year-old, standing nervously. We quickly invited him in and ushered him to Jay's office.

Marcus let us know that he had confused the start time and had arrived two hours earlier, long before we had arrived. Bethany rented its sanctuary and some offices to an Oromo (an ethnic minority within the country of Ethiopia) congregation, and he had arrived in the midst of their worship service. Bethany's process of declaring themselves welcoming to LGBTQ people, as well as hiring Jay, had caused a bit of tension with the more conservative Oromo congregation. However, Jay and the congregation navigated that tension carefully. The Oromo let Marcus know that they were not the LGBTQ youth group and pointed him to the signs that had the correct time listed. Marcus could have given up at that point. He had already driven up from the outer suburbs, and he really wanted to attend, so he decided to wait two hours until the correct time.

We didn't really have a curriculum or a plan for this first meeting. We didn't even expect anyone to show up. We knew that we wanted the focus of the group to be on the youth, so we peppered Marcus with questions. Where was he from? (As previously stated, the city's outer suburbs.) What grade was he in school? (Junior.) How did his family treat him? (They weren't rejecting him, but they were a little uncomfortable and unsure of how to best parent him.) How was his school? (It was fine.) How was his church? (It didn't talk about sexuality all that much.)

We were trying to engage Marcus in conversation, or at least get an idea of what his situation was like, but we sounded like we were interrogating him. He wanted to come to talk to other LGBTQ youth but found himself answering questions from two adults instead. He was our only youth in that first meeting. But we chalked his attendance up as a win and vowed to continue.

If you are going to create a ministry program focused on LGBTQ youth, it is essential that your group meets the actual needs of the LGBTQ youth in your area. We learned that what we want as a minister or as a congregation cannot be what drives an LGBTQ youth ministry. The vision I had in my head is not what we ultimately created, but we were able to find where our vision and the needs of the community overlapped. You will need to spend a lot of time researching your context, both the congregation and the community.

First, focus on the congregation. Many of the following questions are adapted from *Building an Inclusive Church: A Welcoming Toolkit 2.0*, published by the Institute for Welcoming Resources.[2] The book is designed to help congregations form a welcome statement that includes LGBTQ people. One of the tools is an assessment to determine how open the congregation is to creating such a welcoming statement and help determine a course of action. If you are going to create an LGBTQ-inclusive ministry, you need the support of the congregation, which is why the questions are relevant here:

- Does the congregation have a mission or welcoming statement that explicitly includes people of all sexual orientations and gender identities?
- Are your clergy in favor of creating a youth ministry that focuses on LGBTQ youth?
- Are you aware of parents or family members of LGBTQ persons in the congregation?
- Are you aware of LGBTQ persons in the congregation?
- Does the congregation welcome/include a diversity of sexual orientations and gender identities?
- Has your congregation engaged with studies on sexuality or gender?
- Is your congregation a member of a denominational region that has declared itself to be "welcoming"?

The openness of the congregation to creating and supporting an LGBTQ-focused youth ministry will be vital to ensure that you have the resources and the support to make such a ministry happen. The other, and perhaps bigger, assessment needs to be what your community is like. Whether your ministry will be considered necessary will be determined by what other options exist for LGBTQ youth. The following are questions for the community:

- Have there been public arguments about LGBTQ issues in your city or state? What subjects were discussed? Laws? Policies? Other attempts to create inclusive programming (like a drag queen story hour)? A local incident that involved LGBTQ people?
- Are there visible and vocal LGBTQ champions or allies in the community?
- Is there visible and vocal opposition to LGBTQ inclusion in the community?

These sorts of questions will let you know about potential opposition from outside the congregation. You do not want to be blindsided with resistance from local leaders; rather, you want to assess the risks and consider how to mitigate them as much as possible. As a religious institution, your ministry may have freedom from governmental interference, but that will not keep anti-LGBTQ activists from trying to halt it. It also doesn't stop formal opposition from within your denomination or larger church body, which may have the power to curtail your ministry. Here are some questions to ask about the need for an LGBTQ-specific youth ministry in your community:

- What is the culture of the local community? Is it generally supportive and progressive, or would your congregation be considered an oasis for LGBTQ youth in a hostile local culture?
- Does your town/city/state have a nondiscrimination policy for people of all sexual orientations and gender identities?
- How many LGBTQ programs exist in your area? Are they designated for adults or youth? What is their focus? Who tends to participate?
- Do the local schools have LGBTQ organizations? What does their programming look like? What questions have youth been voicing?

You may come to find that your congregation could be a necessary "safe space" for LGBTQ youth in your community and that the ministry will be sorely needed as a way for youth to recharge and center themselves in the midst of a hostile environment.

You may also find that your LGBTQ-specific youth ministry is competing with several other such programs. The intersection of LGBTQ youth and faith may be better accomplished through worship and an inclusive youth ministry rather than something designed exclusively for LGBTQ youth.

This brings me to an important point that you must remember through your visioning process: LGBTQ youth ministry is a niche ministry. This seems obvious, but let me provide a word of warning.

Churches and ministers have seen our program. They decide they want to replicate our LGBTQ youth ministry in some way, but they don't realize how hard it is to recruit youth and sustain a program. I believe that sometimes, youth ministers think the way I did: "If I put together enough of a program, the youth will appear." Know that if you want to create an exclusive youth ministry, you will first spend significant time, energy, and effort simply trying to recruit young people to participate.

This outreach is what takes the bulk of my attention, energy, and effort during the course of the year. Running the week of camp is easy compared to the constant social media posts, mailings, online ads, and emails I produce and the personal outreach I do to raise awareness of The Naming Project. It is a never-ending cycle of recruiting and engaging with young people to maintain a critical mass to keep our program going forward.

When people ask how many campers we have at our annual summer camp, I let them know that it's somewhere between fifteen and twenty campers. They sometimes pause and respond, "That's it? I thought you'd have more than that." I have to explain that our program is very specific. These youth need to be tied to the LGBTQ community. They need to be interested in religion or spirituality. They need to be out enough to ask their parents to sign a permission slip. When all those factors are put together, there aren't enough youth to fill one national camp, let alone several small individual youth ministries.

The first Naming Project summer camp had ten campers, about five times the attendance at our weekly meetings. We thought that the camp would feed attendance at the weekly meetings, which had, quite frankly, been lagging.

After all, now that these youth had such a hard time saying goodbye to each other, the meetings would be an opportunity to reconnect and keep those relationships alive.

We resumed the weekly meetings, being sure to invite all the local youth who had attended the camp (which was most of them that first year). I created a schedule, assigned adult leaders, and listed discussion topics and schedules just the way that I had before we held our first camp.

But it didn't work out as we planned. Some of our youth lived too far away to participate in a two-hour meeting on Sunday afternoons. For those who did live close, returning from camp meant returning to their regular, everyday lives. Youth have very full lives, and LGBTQ youth are no exception. Many students wanted to be there, but play rehearsals, sports, jobs, and other social engagements usually took priority over a meeting in a church basement, even if they still were supportive of a program existing.

We once peaked at five youth all in the same room at the same time. Most weeks, we had a single youth chatting with two adults. We had a core group that was interested and returned on a semiregular basis. The ones who attended the meetings before the camp would return when they could, but our attendance was getting smaller and smaller. Eventually, it was just the two adult leaders talking to each other for two hours.

After a while, we realized that the time and energy we were putting into the weekly meetings were providing less and less value with every passing week with no youth. After a couple of years, we shut down the meetings in order to focus our energy and attention on the summer camp, which was becoming more popular, and on educating others about effective ministry with LGBTQ youth.

I felt as if the weekly meeting program that I had the most direct part in building had failed. I mourned the loss of what I considered my one original idea—and then recognized that the vision had translated into a different reality.

Even with the weekly meetings shut down, recruiting for the camp remained a challenge. I had assumed that building a quality program meant that youth would flock to our camp. The reality is that advertising and recruiting for camp was a challenge in the first year—and still is. We sent out information to every personal contact we knew. Teachers, pastors, youth ministry folks, and parents all got a letter and a brochure—and often an email or call. We asked our small group of weekly meeting participants to sign up and encourage their friends to sign up.

If you are considering an LGBTQ-specific ministry, know that recruiting youth participation will never not be a challenge, and be prepared to put in a lot of effort to make your program work. Because of the ongoing challenge to compete with all the demands on LGBTQ youths' lives, my recommendation is that most youth ministries should include LGBTQ youth but not be exclusively focused on them. Unless you assess that your community has a specific need and demand for a safe place for LGBTQ youth, you are likely to frustrate yourself in the same way that I did.

If you determine that your congregation is a welcoming and open place, then you are likely ministering to LGBTQ youth and adults as well as a variety of family configurations. Of course, LGBTQ youth should absolutely be welcomed. Heteronormativity in youth ministry should be challenged constantly. And yet there may not be a need for a set-apart space. Local LGBTQ organizations may be meeting youths' need for a more exclusive community. And when they need to get away, programs like The Naming Project can supplement the regular ministry they are getting through the congregation.

I am not writing this to throw a wet blanket on your visions for ministry with LGBTQ youth. On the contrary, I simply want you to be "wise as serpents and innocent as doves," as Jesus cautioned.[3] Doing some creative visioning and discernment will give you an expansive idea for ministry that goes beyond the bounds of what has been done before. Careful research and analysis of your community and context will ensure that you are doing this ministry for young people and not for yourself.

I end this chapter with a word of encouragement: The simple act of exploring how best to minister with LGBTQ youth is evidence of your alliance with the community and of your faithfulness to the gospel. Your ministry will be impactful if it reaches even one LGBTQ youth with the message that God's love for them is unfailing. You will have advanced your mission if any non-LGBTQ people learn more about how to be faithful allies to LGBTQ youth in their lives. Continue to dream, to research, and to practice holy hospitality with the LGBTQ youth in your congregation and in your community.

CHAPTER

4

HOW MUCH SHOULD WE FOCUS ON ISSUES OTHER THAN SEXUAL ORIENTATION AND GENDER IDENTITY?

Youth, whether they are LGBTQ or not, are not defined simply by their sexual orientation or gender identity. They have overlapping and intersecting aspects of their identity. The Naming Project is designed with a focus on sexual orientation, gender identity, and faith, but our participants have also been affected by experiences of racism, poverty, and ableism and struggles with mental and emotional health. We cannot simply exclude any of these other aspects of their identity while we focus on them as LGBTQ youth. Their being LGBTQ is not the source of all their problems, nor is it the entirety of their identity.

One of our participants, Landon, was bullied in his small town for being a gay teenage boy. In order to escape the bullying, his parents put him into an alternative school. The students at the alternative school didn't bully him for being gay, but they were a bad influence. They exposed Landon to drugs, which then sent him into a cycle of addiction, treatment, and relapse.

He came to our summer camp in the middle of that cycle. During his first week at our summer camp, Landon went through a huge emotional journey.

He arrived at camp with a lot of baggage from his everyday life, and he wasn't afraid to speak about it with others. Throughout the week, he talked about being bullied and his struggle with drugs. He was also suffering from some mental health problems.

Landon was at times an attention- and energy-demanding ringleader and at other times a sullen loner. When Landon was on, he and the other campers would amplify each other's energy to a manic state. But when we ate at meals, he would sit in a corner by himself, far from the rest of the group. Other campers noticed and called over to him to join them. At one point, one of the counselors made him join the rest of the group, but he only sat in silence and stared off into the distance.

Landon confessed, "When I get into my depressed mood swing, I always want to go off and sit alone. But when I'm alone, all I can do is hope that someone will come over and talk to me."

The week of camp was an escape for Landon because it got him out of the rut he was experiencing in his everyday life. He realized that some of his friends were bad influences, but he hadn't yet found a new group that could support him in developing healthy habits. The campers represented a potential new friend network and support system.

But Landon also knew this group was only together for one week. On Friday, we would all disband and return to our schools and communities. His struggles and temptations would still be there when he returned. While our community was affirming for him as a gay boy, we weren't equipped to deal with mental health struggles or addiction. What we could do was care for, pray for, and affirm him and try to connect him with resources that could help in other aspects of his life.

Landon was a writer who channeled his moods into poems and songs. Some of his poems were morbid, talking about death or being alone. During the camp week, a camera was set up in one of the empty cabins. The campers were invited to go in and say whatever they wanted directly into the camera, like a video diary. The staff jokingly referred to it as the "confessional." Landon would go into the cabin and read his poetry to the camera, but he didn't share his work with the rest of the campers until much later in the week.

We started our last night with a talent show, which we dubbed the "Coffee House Cabaret." We had warned the campers that the Coffee House Cabaret was coming, even including "poetry/music/reading that you would like to share at a 'coffee house'" in the list of items to pack for camp. The performances consisted of songs, dances, and a lot of poetry. After each act, the campers and counselors clapped and cheered with wild abandon to show their affirmation and support for their peers.

Landon prepared one of his poems. He had shared that he originally wrote it when he was depressed, and he often read it when he was depressed. The fact that he was telling the rest of the group about his mood swings was something of a seminal moment for Landon, and we were unsure if he would be able to stand in front of his peers and share a part of himself with them or if he would shun the spotlight and retreat into himself. It was the dichotomy he had described earlier of wanting to sit by himself but also wanting people to come talk to him. His uncertainty about reading his poem was not a fear of rejection but more a fear of vulnerability.

It could be very easy to pin this struggle on Landon's being gay. But the reality is that the mental health issues with which he struggled, ones that I can't identify because I'm not a mental health expert, are common to youth across the board.

Finally, Landon asked another camper to read his poem for him while he sat in the audience. When the recitation ended, everyone clapped and cheered. Some yelled out his name. People recognized what a significant step it was for him to participate in this community with such vulnerability. And Landon beamed.

The encouragement that happens at our camp often transcends affirmation of sexual orientation or gender identity. The people in our community want to support one another as whole people. So, for example, we challenged our campers to look beyond the circle of people in our community and to look beyond themselves, to understand where injustice is happening in the world.

Because they are LGBTQ, our campers are very aware of discrimination against LGBTQ people. However, we wanted them to see the world with the same lens of justice for other communities, ones whose identities they may not share.

I often saw our work as a series of concentric circles. We started our camp week with the message that LGBTQ youth were created, known, and loved by God. This is the message they were expecting and often the reason they participated in our ministry. Some of them needed to hear that message just to understand their own value and worth in the world.

But we also didn't want to leave them in a place where they thought that creation and redemption applied only to them personally, or to their little group, and to no one else. We needed to move the idea of grace and redemption beyond the personal. Often, our camp theme moved from the self, to interpersonal relationships, to communities of school or church, and eventually to the wider world. This ending pushed them to seek out justice for those who weren't as fortunate as they were. To recognize that others were seeking the same affirmation and purpose that they had found at this camp enlarged their minds and hearts and got them thinking beyond their own needs, hurts, and desires.

One of the rules we established at The Naming Project was that "swearing, profanity, or the use of any language which is demeaning to God's creation, especially other people, is never appropriate." When we explained the rule, we put the focus on the "language which is demeaning to God's creation, especially other people" aspect. On one level, this rule is about swearing. We realize that campers and staff will use swear words to make a point or to express their feelings. However, we drew a distinction between self-expression and dishonoring God's creation. This allowed us to have a larger conversation about how our words can be demeaning when we talk about each other and to each other.

Sometimes, such talk of intersectionality was new to the campers, and it pushed them outside of their comfort zone. We have had to confront our youth about their jokes that are based on racism, letting them know that such language is demeaning and trying to get them to understand that they need to be sensitive to racist language, that racism is coded into a lot of our lives, and that even "ironic racist jokes" are still racist.

Our campers are incredibly sensitive to anti-LGBTQ language. They have heard it. They have internalized it. If, however, they are white, male, cisgender, able-bodied, or any other form of dominant culture, they have not been trained in that same level of sensitivity to and scrutiny of racist, sexist, ableist, or any other form of bigoted language.

Beyond just establishing a rule, we structured several aspects of our programming to teach campers how to be proactive in exploring systemic injustice. The large group Bible study themes often bridged into issues of social justice in the current culture because we wanted the Bible study to reflect and be applicable to the world around our youth.

One year, Counselor Logan had just returned from participating in a counterwitness to the white supremacist rally in Charlottesville, Virginia. They (Logan is nonbinary and genderqueer and uses *they* pronouns) had witnessed a lot of the violence firsthand, and they were still processing their experiences and how those experiences impacted them. As we were planning some of our large group Bible studies, we talked about the concentric circles. Logan agreed to talk to the youth about their experience at Charlottesville. This was a big step for us. Most of our campers were white, some came from sheltered backgrounds, and some didn't know enough about what had even happened. Logan had to craft a narrative that helped explain racism in America, how it was playing out in this specific instance, and their own personal experience and perspective—all while fitting it into our overall Bible study theme of being "fully alive." It was a hard task, and Logan did it well, being both vulnerable and honest. The youth listened attentively.

One girl raised her hand and said, "I don't know the best way to word this question, so I'm sorry if it comes off as disrespectful. But our president said that there were some 'very fine people on both sides.' Do you think that the police who were there were working to protect both sides?"

The counselors were in awe. We thought that this question demonstrated a deep awareness of and sensitivity to the world around us. She connected Logan's story with what she had already heard in the news, finding the points of discrepancy and gently asking about them.

And yet our campers aren't always so astute. During a different session, another counselor, Greg, took the campers through an activity that made them explore wealth distribution. He scattered pennies all over the floor and told the campers to grab as many as they could. Of course, some got more than others. The activity and the discussion surrounding it reflected the national discussion of wealth inequality. Some campers, particularly those who blocked others and snatched up as many coins as they could, wanted a system that would protect their pile of pennies. Some suggested a shared wealth model.

But the overall tone was one of anger at Greg for coming up with the activity. Some campers asked why we would introduce an activity that caused division and strife among the tight group of campers. Others complained the activity was a failure because it led to awkward questions and tense discussions. The campers said they were looking for a caring and safe space, and a difficult discussion about wealth inequality was making it less caring and less safe.

Despite the campers labeling the activity a "failure," having a hard conversation about a difficult topic was necessary. What makes our campers understand intersectionality is having the issue brought to them. If they are sheltered from any form of difficult discussion, they never learn how to navigate difference.

Our job isn't to make their lives easy but to equip them to handle the difficult complexities of life. Sometimes the topics and discussions resonate personally with our youth, and other times, we bring them up so that the youth can be aware of the intersecting world around them. Sometimes, the issues we raise resonate well with campers.

CHAPTER

5

HOW JESUS-Y SHOULD OUR PROGRAM BE?

Before the first Naming Project summer church camp launched, we were nervous. We wondered what this experience would be like for our ten youth. Would they find us too Jesus-y? Not Jesus-y enough? Would they find our activities and discussions elementary and simplistic or too theologically complex? We had no idea what to expect.

By that point, we had run our weekly meetings for a year, and we knew some of the youth who would be attending. We were most curious about Autumn. Autumn attended a local church and had participated in a few of the weekly meetings we held. She had grown up attending a church camp in Minnesota, and when she was old enough to be a junior counselor, she was told that she wasn't allowed to talk about sexuality. She couldn't talk about herself or her bisexual identity even if the campers asked. If she did, she would be accused of encouraging homosexuality among the campers. Perhaps as a result of this experience, or because she was naturally entering adolescence, Autumn had a lot of questions and doubts about her faith. She had already talked about taking a step back from the faith of her childhood and was openly wondering what sort of church camp The Naming Project might be. She knew our camp was specifically designed to welcome and affirm LGBTQ youth, but she questioned if it would still have an altar call or threats of hell if campers didn't accept Christ into their hearts the way other camps had.

We had no intention of holding an altar call or any "conversion" moment in our camp program, but that fear lingered for Autumn—and probably for several other campers—before they arrived. The fear was well founded. Many Christian camps, as well as retreats and even weekly services, include a long evening worship time that through music and preaching aims to elicit particular emotions of vulnerability and contrition that lead up to some form of an "altar call" moment, when people are asked to present themselves, pray a very specific prayer, and "let Jesus into their heart." It is a standard practice at many evangelical functions.

I personally had my own discomfort with altar calls. I had witnessed several. One of my early dates with Richard, who would later become my husband, was visiting the evangelical church he attended. We approached the end of a long service that involved loud and high-energy music, a sermon, and then songs designed to make people cry. The altar call came after people had gone through an emotional process, when they were feeling the most vulnerable. Since this was my first religious outing with Richard, I was scared he would push me up there and make me participate.[1]

Elsewhere, I had heard conversion talked about like it was godly score keeping. When I worked at the youth and family institute after college, our executive director told me a story about a meeting with evangelical pastors who asked him how many people he had converted. He was quick, responding that he doesn't convert anyone through his preaching or actions alone but that conversion is the work of the Holy Spirit. He reported to us, with a glint in his eye, that the pastors looked at him blankly and said, "So zero, then?"

I had even heard one of my more evangelical colleagues in youth ministry describe evangelism as trying to get "more people on our side." I was having a particularly hard day, so I responded with, "It's not our side. It's God's side, and some days I even wonder if I'm on God's side. So maybe I need to work on myself more than on anyone else." I felt that the popular attention on conversion was short term and shallow, not helpful to anyone's long-term journey of faith.

I wasn't alone. All the founding leaders of The Naming Project were Lutheran, and all shared my discomfort that a "conversion moment" was necessary for salvation. We believed that God created everything that exists, including each one of us. God has gifted us with redemption without our earning it or asking for it. And God already takes up dwelling in our hearts, whether we choose to acknowledge it or not. We were not arrogant enough to believe that we somehow controlled God's action in the world or in the hearts and minds of the campers and counselors.

Our camp was going to be a tiring, emotional process. We knew that because camps always are. We didn't want to manipulate our campers by using that exhaustion and emotional energy so that we could claim to have "converted them." We would present a camp with Christian themes that would manifest themselves in the Bible study discussion, worship, and campfire songs, but there would be no pressure for anyone to declare their faith. Instead, our focus was on letting the youth discover and live into their faith just as they would discover their sexual orientation or gender identity—for themselves.

As leaders, we drew on decades-old songs and activities that we remembered doing during our own time as campers, even as far back to our own elementary school years. And yet the faithfulness to the tradition from which we came made our camp programming much more effective. The fact was that in those first years, we were a Lutheran camp, and it made sense for us to act Lutheran—to be as authentically ourselves as possible.

During the first campfire, Pastor Brad Froslee, who originated the idea of an LGBTQ church camp with The Naming Project, led the youth through a ritual that reminded me of one of my earliest memories from being at church camp. Brad talked about the ills of the world, of society, and of our own lives. "Within the Christian tradition," he said, "we label that as sin." As he was talking, another adult leader named Lauren dragged out a large wooden cross on a stand and placed it by the campfire while I handed out small pieces of paper and markers. Brad instructed us to write tangible examples of the ills of the world, a burden we were carrying, or something that was concerning us. We then impaled the pieces of paper onto nails on the cross. The papers layered over one another, forming a stack of sin. Then while Brad proclaimed an absolution, Jay lit the papers on fire. If you have never seen this ritual before, it makes a compelling visual image. The papers turn black and curl in on themselves as they burn. What remains bears a resemblance to a black rose. Brad reminded us that in dying on the cross, Jesus took the sins and burdens of the world, things that are harsh and ugly, and turned them into something beautiful, like a rose.

Looking back on it, the ritual is somewhat simplistic, complicated to set up during a campfire, and quite frankly, a little hokey. But it is also effective.

When we expanded our leadership beyond Lutherans, we encouraged adult leaders from other denominations to be as authentic to their traditions as possible. That meant that we had strands of our program that were more evangelical, more Baptist, more Unitarian, more Episcopal, and sometimes more secular. Counselors led various portions of the camp, using the language and rituals with which they were most comfortable.

I was mildly surprised to find that our youth participants, who also came from a range of faith backgrounds (and occasionally, a background of no faith), not only were open to the Jesus-y songs, prayers, and rituals but eagerly participated in them. We even had campers who readily identified themselves as agnostic or atheist, and yet they sang songs like "Sanctuary" with full-throated abandon.

During one of our weekly meetings, one of our regulars, Marcus, brought his boyfriend, Luke. Marcus warned us beforehand that his new boyfriend practiced Wicca and said, "Don't scare him away by being too Jesus-y." We checked in with Luke when we started the program to make sure he would be comfortable, and he assured us he was fine. Luke's first visit corresponded with a Bible study on the book of Luke, which led to jokes that he had shown up at just the right time. As we got going with the Bible study, I was monitoring Luke's reactions. I didn't want to overwhelm him with anything that was too in-depth, but I didn't need to worry. Luke asked some great questions about Luke and the Bible as a whole. Who wrote the book of Luke? Why is Luke different from other books that tell similar stories about Jesus? Why do certain writings make it into the Bible while others are left out? Why do Christians see the Bible as so authoritative? His questions were genuine and from a place of personal interest. Instead of frightening Luke, we seemed to be giving him a glimpse into Christianity that differed from the judgmental, homophobic version he had witnessed most in our culture.

I wanted to get a sense of what Luke thought of our program and of this view of Christianity, so I invited him out to coffee on a weekday afternoon. I wanted to get his assessment of The Naming Project, especially as someone who identified outside of Christianity. Luke seemed very happy that his boyfriend had found a place to support him spiritually. He told me he had come to our meeting to support Marcus but ended up enjoying the discussion.

Midway through the conversation, I said, "I don't really know much about Wicca, and I wanted to hear what it means to you."

"I like it because it's such an earth-based religion. It's tangible and tied to the actual world around us," Luke responded. "I used to be more into it, but I haven't been as involved lately. I've gotten more into property development."

I smiled, realizing that Luke was asking the same questions other youth are: Who am I? What do I believe? What am I going to do with my life? Those questions can be answered by religions like Wicca or Christianity but also with career choices, activities, and in Luke's case, property development.

What this taught me was that we only have to offer a faithful experience to the best of our ability. The rest is between the youth we have in our presence and the Holy Spirit. We cannot force a youth to believe the same way we do, but we can openly and authentically represent our faith and the tradition from which we come. The youth who should be there will be there, and they will be more open than we anticipate.

Our youth are from a larger and wider cloud of witnesses than just our youth ministry community. That cloud of witnesses may include churches they are from or churches to which they will go in the future. While The Naming

Project or your ministry cannot be anyone's entire life of faith, it can be an important part of it.

What LGBTQ youth need are supportive systems in every area of their lives—ones that accept them for who they are, listen to them, believe what they tell us about themselves, equip them to deal with the challenges that exist out in the world, and challenge them to be ambassadors for the love of Christ to a world that isn't ready to hear it.

And occasionally, the Holy Spirit will use us to reach someone in a new and unexpected way.

CHAPTER

6

WHAT DO LGBTQ YOUTH WANT TO BE CALLED?

Sapiosexual.
Genderfluid.
Demisexual.
Nonbinary.
Agender.
Skoliosexual.

The universe of terms to describe sexual orientations and gender identities is ever expanding, and it can be easy as a youth minister, parent, or just an older adult to feel as if young—and specifically, young LGBTQ—people are speaking a completely new language. Perhaps you feel intimidated or overwhelmed by terms that you've never heard before and don't completely understand.

It's OK that you don't know. Language around LGBTQ people is constantly evolving, and there is no inherent way to learn something new without taking a little time to do research.[1]

The terms used to describe the LGBTQ community were once assigned by people outside the community. *Homosexual* was the most commonly used word used to describe anyone who wasn't heterosexual (or straight) and cisgender. A German psychologist named Karoly Maria Benkerta, who was studying LGBTQ people in the nineteenth century, coined the term.[2] In short, LGBTQ people did not create it; an outside (heterosexual) observer did.

Over time, members of the community wanted to claim words about themselves for themselves and to define who they were rather than to be defined by someone else. So they began using other words to describe themselves: *gay*, *lesbian*, *bisexual*, and *transgender*. They even reclaimed the former slur *queer*.

So let's take a moment to unpack some of the most common phrases you might hear. This will not be an exhaustive list, and it's always worthwhile to look up the nuances, but it'll get you started.

First, everyone has a sexual orientation. *Sexual orientation* refers to the feelings you have about others—that is, the gender of a person whom you find attractive, with whom you want to get romantic or sexy. Some of the most common sexual orientations are gay, lesbian, bisexual, asexual, and heterosexual, or straight. Yes, straight people also have a sexual orientation. It is not a term exclusively for LGBTQ people.

Second, everyone has a gender identity. This is about yourself—your deep, innate understanding of who you are in terms of gender. When you examine yourself and your feelings, do you see yourself as masculine? Feminine? Something in between? Something other? Only you know your gender identity. It's not something that can be seen externally but something you know innately. If how you understand yourself matches with the way you are perceived externally (especially by the doctor who is filling out your birth certificate), then you are considered *cisgender* (*cis* is Latin for "on the same side as"). If the way you understand yourself doesn't match how you are perceived by others (especially the doctor who is filling out your birth certificate), then you are considered *transgender* (*trans* is Latin for "crossing over"). Someone can be transgender without ever telling anyone or doing anything about it. They do not need medical procedures or legal documentation. The moment they know that there is incongruence between what they know about themselves and what the world assumes about their gender, they are transgender.

Transgender is an umbrella term and has many permutations and nuances. Besides *cisgender* and *transgender*, you might hear terms like *genderfluid*, *genderqueer*, *nonbinary*, or *agender*. As you learn more about the youth with whom you work, you may get more specific. Just as there isn't one color that is yellow—the designation encompasses many shades and hues—there are many ways to be transgender . . . just like there are many ways to be cisgender.

Which leads us to the term *gender expression*. No matter how we feel about our gender internally, we do several things to express our gender so others can pick up on the cues and more safely and accurately make assumptions about our gender identity. Our name, pronouns, clothing, hairstyle, tone of voice, gait, posture, and so much more give people hints about how they should interpret our gender identity. The conventions that make up *masculine*, *feminine*, and even the more general term *gender nonconforming* are all culturally specific. As little as one hundred years ago, pink, a color we quickly associate with girls, was perceived as a much more manly color. Why? Because pink was a toned-down version of red, and red was considered the color of war.[3] What is considered masculine today in the United States is not the same as what was considered masculine two hundred years ago in a different country.

Gender expression is also contextual. Someone who is transgender—whose self-understanding doesn't match how they are perceived by the outside world, which often sees only "manly men" and "girly girls"—may dress in a way that signals, "I'm not what you assume. I'm wearing clothes and sporting a haircut that tells you that I do not match the letter the doctor wrote on my birth certificate." However, many people live in a place where transgressing gender norms may be dangerous or even deadly. They must, out of necessity, express their gender in a way that doesn't draw attention or lead them to be attacked. This is why gender expression is different from gender identity. Gender identity is internal and immutable. However, gender expression is something over which we have much more control, and people choose to exercise that control when they are in a place where they can share themselves with the world physically, emotionally, and spiritually.

To recap: Everyone has a sexual orientation. Everyone has a gender identity. And everyone expresses that gender in a different way, known as gender expression. These three things are independent of one another. People will identify themselves, form relationships (or not) with the type(s) of people they find attractive, and express their gender in the way that balances authenticity and personal safety.

There are quite literally hundreds of possible ways those three factors could combine in an individual. This is why people are looking for more precise terms with which to describe themselves. If this seems complicated, it is. The United States has never had a reliable number of how many people compose the LGBTQ community. LGBTQ people have not been counted in the census. Gallop, the polling company, has written about how complicated it is to measure the LGBTQ community,[4] even while the company places the LGBTQ community between 4 to 5 percent of the US population.[5] The most common popular assumption was around 10 percent. GLAAD's 2017 Accelerating Acceptance survey, however, found that as many as 20 percent of eighteen- to thirty-four-year olds (the youngest group polled) identified in some way under the wide umbrella of the LGBTQ community, a percentage that was much higher than previously estimated.[6] Why is that number so high compared to all the most recent estimates? The respondents aren't simply identifying as gay, bisexual, lesbian, queer, or even LGBTQ. Instead, this 20 percent identifies as "not strictly heterosexual and not strictly cisgender." The actual terms LGBTQ persons use to describe themselves are complicated and getting broader all the time.

Why is that?

As LGBTQ people are more broadly understood and accepted, they want to be more precise about the language that describes them and their realities in the world. For some, *gay* doesn't accurately describe their feelings, attractions, and relationships. Some of these words have connotations of white exclusivity or male dominance. Some are considered too binary for a world with a plethora of ways to live and identify, so more terms are constantly being created. As young people learn more about themselves, they will research if there are words that describe how they feel and perceive themselves. They may try on one or more terms until they find the one that fits.

In a 2018 interview with *Rolling Stone* magazine, actor and singer Janelle Monáe described how she learned new words to identify her sexual orientation. Though initially she identified as bisexual, Monáe told the magazine, "Later I read about pansexuality and was like, 'Oh, these are things that I identify with too.' I'm open to learning more about who I am."[7]

Monáe's experience with self-discovery and learning new words mirrors that of many LGBTQ youth. I spoke to a young transgender woman who told me a very similar story. From her preschool through her Pentecostal university, she grew up in an insulated family and controlling environment. Everyone treated her as a boy, but her feelings and self-understanding weren't matching what she was being told by her family, doctors, counselors, pastors, and even university leaders. She told me that when she encountered the word *transgender* for the first time, it was as if something fell into place—an experience of "Oh, *that's* what I've been feeling for so long!" Learning the language was the first step toward understanding more fully who she was and living into her identity.

Think about it: LGBTQ people are not born with an inherent language to describe how they feel and how they perceive themselves. Every word and phrase they know about identity has to be taught to them, and most of these are based on an assumed heterosexuality and cisgender identity. Youth who are LGBTQ have to learn what an LGBTQ word or phrase means and then understand to what extent that term matches how they understand themselves. When there doesn't seem to be a word that describes how they feel, they do what we all do with the English language: they make up a new word that better describes who they are.

As a youth minister, you may be getting worried that you cannot possibly keep up with this ever-expanding dictionary. It can feel like the vocabulary quizzes we faced in school. But I have good news for you: If a young person in your ministry shares a term that you are unfamiliar with, simply tell them you haven't heard that word before. Then ask them to define it in their own words. Rather than learning a dictionary definition of any term, you should learn these terms through a relationship with someone that you know, someone you trust, someone you care about. That way, when you hear that word in the future, you don't panic and try to recall the "right" definition; you recall the face of the person who first taught you the term.

Now is not the time to dismiss or negate what the youth are telling you. Now is the time to listen and learn. If you have questions, make them clarifying (not challenging) questions. Treat every new term as a stepping stone toward learning more about the young person in front of you. That person is your most immediate concern, but they are also a little window into understanding a vast and diverse LGBTQ community. You have the opportunity to learn along with the youth.

"But," you might be asking, "each person is so unique and special. No term is universal. What can I call each individual LGBTQ youth that lets them know they are seen and known and loved?"

There is something you can call youth that will speak directly to them as individual people: their preferred name. It's what you'd want for yourself, isn't it?

CHAPTER

7

WHAT IS THE BIG DEAL ABOUT NAMES?

Consider your own name. How come you were given that name? Were you named after someone? How many middle names do you have, and why, and what are they? Do you like your given name? Do you go by a nickname? Was that nickname given to you, or was it something you adopted for yourself?

Names have always been viewed as very powerful. Several cultures have an elaborate naming ceremony in which the newborn (or in some cultures, not-so-newborn) child is given a name.

The power of names is exemplified in Scripture. Biblical characters' names are deeply tied to their identity. On Easter morning, Mary Magdalene goes to visit the body of Jesus and discovers that it is missing. In her grief, the risen Jesus approaches her and talks to her. She doesn't recognize him. She thinks that he is the gardener and that he has removed Jesus's body for some reason. She doesn't even recognize that she is speaking to Jesus. But upon hearing her name spoken aloud, Mary finally realizes that the one speaking to her is a dear friend and teacher.

Names are also changed frequently in the Bible, especially at points of new identity and destiny. Biblical characters have their names changed when the direction of their lives changes: Abram becomes Abraham, Sarai becomes Sarah, Jacob becomes Israel, Saul becomes Paul. Their new names signal a major life change.

In Scripture, the new name is proclaimed at a moment of high drama. In Matthew 16, Jesus asks the disciples how he is perceived and understood by others who don't know him as well as they do. This feeling is also relatable to LGBTQ youth, who are constantly navigating how they are perceived. They wonder, Do people know I'm gay? Will they accept me as bisexual? What are people saying about the way I look or dress or act?

The disciples give Jesus some answers to describe how the crowds perceive him. And then Jesus asks what is probably the most vulnerable and difficult question someone can ask of his friends: "Who do *you* say that I am?"[1] Jesus is no longer interested in the opinions of the crowds and the strangers. He wants to know how his closest companions, those who have lived and worked with him the most intimately, understand him. The opinions of those who are closest to us are the ones that matter the most. We can ignore or avoid the negativity of the masses, but rejection from family or friends is devastating. On the other hand, having just *one* supportive adult in their life can reduce the likelihood that an LGBTQ youth will attempt suicide by 40 percent.[2]

Simon responds to Jesus's question, "You are the Christ, the Son of the living God."

Imagine what a relief this is for Jesus. He feels seen and recognized. Simon has seen past the labels society has placed on Jesus. He has really looked and listened to who Jesus is and has taken all that to heart.

Jesus responds to Simon's affirmation of who he is with both a blessing and a new name. Simon becomes Peter, or "rock" in Greek. The name isn't random; it is a calling and a destiny. Jesus proclaims, "Upon this Rock I will build my church." The new name meant something significant. It wasn't the name that Peter's parents gave to him; it was one that looked forward to who he was becoming.

Most LGBTQ youth, especially transgender youth, can relate to biblical stories of name changes on a deep and personal level. A name change for transgender youth is a milestone, one that marks the transition from the person they have been perceived as to the person they are discovering themselves to be. Some youth will try out a variety of names, trying to figure out what name fits them. They are learning and discovering who they are rather than who they are told to be, and they want a name that reflects their true identity.

One youth tried on different names over the years of attending our summer camp. In the first year of attending, the youth was using the girl's name given to him by his parents at his birth. The next year, he asked to simply be called J, the first letter of his old name. He was deeply concerned about making it easy for everyone to remember not to use his former name. He chose J because he thought it might be easier for the group, not necessarily because of how he felt the name J matched his identity. He actually apologized to us for asking us to recognize him by his new name. We all assured him that we would do everything in our power to call him J during our week together.

The next year, he returned as Noah. He said the name Noah was one he had always liked, and he thought it fit him pretty well. He said it might not be the name he uses for the rest of his life, but he wanted to be able to test it in a safe environment. Like the year before, we all adjusted, and he continued to use that name.

Noah's idea of "trying on" new names is a little different from how we hear about the sudden name changes in Scripture, but the idea of a name being a way to allow you to be seen and understood in your new or full identity resonates well with the many examples of this we see in the Bible.

Imagine a young person who knows at every instance that the name they are called doesn't reflect who they truly are. They have trained themselves to respond to it, but every time they hear it, they feel as if it is directed at someone else. When they do find the name that fits, it marks a change in their life. The new name may accompany other elements of transition, such as changes in clothing and hairstyles. The name change, along with the changing gender expression, lets other people see them as they see and understand themselves.

Young people who came to our ministry were figuring out who they were. They were exploring names with which they identified and determining which ones didn't fit. Our youth ministry became focused on identity, as signified by our focus on names.

When Jay and I were starting this new youth ministry program, we wrote a grant proposal to attempt to get some start-up money. We opened with the line, "The purpose of (*NAME*) is to. . . ." The name we couldn't decide upon we made all caps, bold, and italic to remind us to fill in this blank.

We continued working on the grant application but kept realizing that we hadn't even come up with a name for the program. We kept staring at the word *NAME*, trying to figure out what to put in that very obvious placeholder. We even joked that we'd just called our new organization *NAME*.

Jay started riffing on the joke, musing about what we were looking at. He said that kids call each other all sorts of names. Some are friendly and intimate nicknames, but some names have a nasty, unkind edge to them, especially for those kids who are different. Kids who are LGBTQ get called all sorts of names—none of them friendly or familiar or affirming.

Fag.
Dyke.
Queer.
Tranny.
Freak.
Deviant.

Most LGBTQ youth have heard these names directed either at them or at someone else. People use them to make LGBTQ people feel inadequate, unhuman, unloved, and unfamiliar.

But God knows each of us by name. What's more, God gives each of us the name "child of God." No matter what names, labels, or slurs the world gives us, the underlying name "child of God" endures.

We mused about what we were planning. Adolescence is a time when we figure out who we are, so the idea of naming really stuck with us. Perhaps the purpose of our program would be to help LGBTQ youth know for themselves the baptismal promise that God knows them by name and calls them by name. Perhaps the young people who would come to our program would be grappling with the names that are being hurled at them. Perhaps they would be figuring out how they wanted to present themselves to the world and by what name they wanted to be known. Given how deeply names are tied to identity and destiny, we thought, Why not call our LGBTQ youth ministry The Naming Project?

CHAPTER

8

HOW CAN THE CHURCH HELP YOUTH WRESTLE WITH IDENTITY QUESTIONS?

In Genesis, Jacob spends his youth cheating and swindling his brother, Esau. He extorts Esau, preying upon Esau's hunger and desperation to take possession of his birthright. He steals Esau's identity, impersonating him before their father and extracting a blessing meant for Esau, and then runs away rather than face the consequences. After years of grifting and hustling, Jacob is about to meet his brother again. This is a moment of reckoning.

The night before Jacob reunites with Esau, Jacob sleeps utterly alone. He sends his servants, his possessions, and even his family on ahead of him. He realizes he cannot hide behind others to avoid his betrayal. Finally Jacob is making himself utterly known and vulnerable.

Out of nowhere, a man appears and wrestles with Jacob. The wrestling match lasts until sunrise, when the mystery man asks Jacob his name. When Jacob provides it, the wrestler responds, "You shall no longer be called Jacob, but Israel, for you have striven with God and with humans, and have prevailed."[1] Israel, formerly known as Jacob, asks the man's name in return, but it is not given. In those days, to know someone's name meant to have power over that person. This mystery wrestler—God—claims Israel as God's own. But God will not be confined or controlled by any human, even Israel.

God created us and knows each one of us by name. God knows who we are and who we are becoming. God creates us with talents and quirks and abilities, and then there are the things that we learn and into which we grow as we live in this world. At its best, when it's doing it right, the church plays a proactive role in identity formation, helping answer that slow-burning question of "Who am I?"

Church rituals formulate a sense of identity. The importance we give to our rituals and how we perform them help shape who we are. In my Lutheran Church, baptism is typically (but not exclusively) performed on infants. As a Lutheran, I believe the promises in baptism are made by God, the parents, and the community around the child. Parents pledge to "live with them among God's faithful people, bring them to the word of God and the holy Supper, teach them the Lord's Prayer, the Creed, and the Ten Commandments, place in their hands the holy scriptures, and nurture them in faith and prayer, so that your children may learn and trust God, proclaim Christ through word and deed, care for others and the world God made, and work for justice and peace."[2] The church community pledges to help and support the parents in fulfilling these promises.

God knew Israel's past, God knew his old name of Jacob, and God wrestled with him. In wrestling with him, God claimed and renamed him Israel as a promise of his future. Knowing someone's name means that you know that person deeply and intimately, that you have wrestled with them. Using the name that matches their identity recognizes their individuality. In baptism, God claims us as his own and gives us the name "child of God." This claim on our lives overrides the claim this world tries to place on us. The name "child of God" is given to us by God in the promise of baptism. It reminds us that God created us and placed us in this world. And through all our living in this world, we are still God's beloved creation.

The church has established many programs and rituals to help the families, the sponsors, and the wider church community fulfill their baptismal promises. We have Sunday school programs, children and youth ministry, a Bible gift program for third graders, and first communion and confirmation classes. Summer camp is another program that churches have used to help fulfill the baptismal promises. The network of Christian camps in the United States serves elementary, junior, and senior high youth. Some churches make camp a part of their confirmation program. The camp I attended as a youth and at which I worked as a college student even designated one week as "confirmation camp" for junior high youth going through the confirmation program. Such camps and programs are designed to help youth claim for themselves the baptismal promises made on their behalf, moving the responsibility for faith formation from the parents to the youth.

In many churches, LGBTQ Christians feel a tension around this process of faith identity formation. On one hand, the church offers rituals and stories that affirm our identity as children of God. These stories and rituals claim that we are made in the image of God and that we are beloved children of God and part of the worshipping community. On the other hand, the perception some church people hold about LGBTQ identity leads them to treat us as something that is outside of the worshipping community. Many churches have been struggling for years with how best to "deal with" LGBTQ people—as if we are a problem to be solved. During the 2000s, the argument revolved around marriage and the ordination of LGBTQ people. While these are important issues, by focusing almost exclusively on them, these denominations overlooked the critical mission of faith formation in young LGBTQ people, who are at the crucial juncture of discovering various aspects of their identity and learning how they all fit together.

Chris was one such youth who spent a lot of time trying to integrate various aspects of his identity. When Chris began to realize he was gay, he knew his orientation would be at odds with his home church community. The dominant message he was hearing was that he could not be a faithful Christian and a gay man at the same time. And this was a message he internalized.

First, Chris threw himself into the church, trying to suppress his gay identity. He joined every group and attended all kinds of retreats and events. As much as possible, he listened only to Christian music and consumed only "Christian" products.

But this running and hiding from the gay part of his identity made him feel as if he was overlooking and neglecting an important part of himself. The reality of his sexual orientation wasn't going to be suppressed. So he then went to the opposite extreme. He stopped attending his church, he stopped listening to Christian radio. But that also didn't feel right. Trying to suppress his faith was just as impossible as suppressing his sexual orientation.

The reality is that both of those aspects of his identity are essential parts of what makes the person we came to know as Chris. And the messages he was receiving, either explicitly or implicitly, about denying a part of himself were stunting his ability to discern who God created him to be and what he was called to do in the world.

Historically, the church has treated LGBTQ people in one of two ways—namely, punitive rejection or ignorance. The punitive rejection takes on forms we can readily recognize as such: condemnatory words from the pulpit, presentations about the so-called dangers of LGBTQ identity, political opposition to laws or policies that would accept LGBTQ people, or attempts to force changes in sexual orientation or gender identity. This rejection affects both adults and youth, whether they are out or still closeted. For teenagers who haven't told anyone about their sexual orientation, these words send the harmful message that the LGBTQ youth was created not in God's image but out of evil. LGBTQ youth then identify with the evil about which the public is warning them regardless of anything they have done—just for being who they are. The secondary message is that the church will not be a safe place for them to be themselves.

Fortunately, the number of Christian leaders who practice punitive rejection is declining, although this experience of church persecution is still horrific for those who endure it. Much more common among church leaders is ignorance. This happens even passively because ignorance reinforces heteronormativity—that is, the belief that heterosexuality and cisgender identity are and should be the only lived realities in their church. It happens through shorthand policy phrases like "Girls are pink. Boys are blue. Don't make purple." It happens through relationship education that focuses only on heterosexual couples. It happens with an awkward response to an LGBTQ coming out or sharing their relationship story.

Your calling to work with LGBTQ youth likely means you are not going to be engaging in punitive rejection. But ignorance will continue to be a challenge. How do you minister to a young person, with all their complex personality, without erasing any part of them? How do you balance the unique perspective and needs of one LGBTQ youth in the midst of the rest of the young people in your ministry? I don't want to underestimate the challenge, but keeping it in your mind will make sure you aren't ignoring any LGBTQ youth.

Remember, you are ministering to a person, a child of God. That child of God is created with talents and quirks. They are also created with a sexual orientation and a gender identity. Young people are figuring out who they are and how they relate to the rest of the world. You seeing youth as a whole people, calling each one by name, and recognizing *all* that God made them to be will remind them that God created them, knows them, and calls each one of them "child of God."

CHAPTER

9

WHAT HOLY DAYS AND RITUALS DO LGBTQ YOUTH OBSERVE? ARE THESE EVEN CHRISTIAN?

Churches know how to do holidays and rituals. The traditional church calendar is built around annual tentpole celebrations of Christmas and Easter with several other holidays in between. Christians have sacraments, liturgy, songs, and special days they enact with a passion that makes these rituals meaningful on a personal and communal level.

Just as the church has established rituals that reinforce identity in Christ, the LGBTQ community has developed some rites of passage, annual commemorations, and rituals that shape our identity. Such holidays are holy days for the LGBTQ community. They bring awareness, they encourage expression, and they are marked by a range of rituals and traditions that can be honed to fit the personal experiences and expressions of each person, bonding them with the larger community of shared identity.

Each June, cities around the world mark Pride. Pride is the most well known of the LGBTQ holy days, and it is filled with story and ritual. Pride is a historical commemoration of the Stonewall riots. In June 1969, New York City police raided the Stonewall Inn. Instead of being hauled away as usual, in front of cameras that could ruin patrons' careers and families, this crowd of largely queer, gender-nonconforming people of color fought back.

The three-day riot wasn't the first instance of LGBTQ people fighting back. But it emboldened the leaders to push for greater visibility and acceptance—for example, by forming much more explicitly queerly named organizations. On the one-year anniversary, advocates marched to commemorate the riots. That march was repeated year after year on the last Sunday in June, and this is what has morphed into the Pride marches of today in cities around the world.

The story of the Stonewall riots is told and retold from various perspectives. Historians attempt to separate the facts from the legend. Some people reverently invoke historical figures who were present at the riots, figures like Sylvia Rivera and Marsha P. Johnson. They discuss and debate the historical advances and setbacks of the LGBTQ community and each of the communities under the larger LGBTQ umbrella. People recount to their friends and loved ones stories of their first Pride celebration. The storytelling is both personal and epic, just like the stories we tell in our congregations, at camps, and elsewhere in the life of the church.

Pride is also a display of ritual. Each year, LGBTQ people and their advocates march down the street. This act serves as a reenactment of the first Christopher Street march in 1970, which was launched to remember the Stonewall riots of the previous year. Over time, the march has become bigger and more widely accepted and has attracted more corporate participation. Many people now describe it as a "parade" rather than the protest from which it originated. Yet with the flurry of rainbows, we also get the think pieces and social media posts that complain that Pride is just a party, that Pride is too corporate, that individuals won't participate because they aren't into "the scene." It's not unlike the complaining we hear in our churches about the commercialism of the Christmas season. And yet we continue to participate, to trek down the street, re-creating the first march, which was done as an act of defiance and visibility within a hostile world. Marching is a ritual that has come to define Pride.

In many ways, Pride is both a look back at how far we've come and a look forward to how much work is ahead of us as a community. What gives us courage is that we do that work as a community and in public.

Holy days such as Pride are secular events that were created at a time when most religious groups were ignoring or actively persecuting the LGBTQ community. So *don't* look for inherent Christian language in the lead-up to or on the day itself. But *do* look for storytelling and ritual. Look for naming and claiming. Look for people sharing with the world a piece of who they are. And look for others surrounding them and letting them know they are accepted and loved, at least by their own community. And look for straight people observing and listening, tentatively participating alongside their loved ones, using the holy days to gain a better understanding of their friends and family. Perhaps you're among them. Perhaps you, as a youth ministry leader, might consider participating in such events as a supporter?

Some people insist that LGBTQ holy days are entirely secular and have nothing to do with the church. Not so. Jeanne Manford walked in one of the first Pride marches with her son, holding a sign that read "Parents of Gays United in Support of Their Children." She was approached by so many young people asking her to speak to their parents, as well as other parents asking how they could support their children, that she established a parents' support group in a local United Methodist Church. Eventually that group became PFLAG, or Parents and Friends of Lesbians and Gays.[1]

There is no reason that your youth group or congregation can't participate in Pride, or any of the LGBTQ holidays, in a way that aligns with your congregation's culture and values. There may be some that are better fits for your congregation than others because of geography, demographics, or congregational history. Some churches along the routes of local Pride walks have offered to provide water to participants, who are often tired and parched from the long (often hot) march.

Your youth group and your congregation are members of a much wider, global commemoration. Just as every family, region, and country celebrate Christmas in a different way, so too can we participate in LGBTQ celebrations, awareness days, and observances with the reverence we bring to an Easter sunrise service, the noise and celebration we bring to Pentecost, or the nostalgic wonder we feel at a Christmas Eve candlelight service. Participate as it feels right and appropriate to you and your congregational culture.

Some LGBTQ religious organizations[2] invite churches to participate in Welcoming Church Sunday on the last Sunday of January. It is an LGBTQ holy day created explicitly for faith communities. Congregations who have stated that they are open to persons of all sexual orientations and gender identities (among others) participate to remind people why their congregation makes a public welcome statement and to explore ways in which to live out that welcome even more fully. Many LGBTQ religious organizations publish liturgical resources to help in planning, but you can work with your youth to make the worship service as queer and fabulous as possible. You could even suggest that this become one of the services in which the youth take as many leadership roles as possible. Invite an LGBTQ youth who is good at public speaking to deliver the homily. Rerender a hymn into a pop song or vice versa. Your imagination and the participation of the rest of the congregation are the only limits.

Some LGBTQ holy days are somber. Transgender Day of Remembrance on November 20 is a memorial service. On that day, we remember transgender people who died by violence. These services are often held in LGBTQ centers and places where there is space for plenty of people to gather, to call out the names of those who were lost, and to pray for an end to violence. As churches, we already know how to do memorial services well. So why not offer your congregational space to the local transgender community on this day? Invite your youth to volunteer to help the memorial service run smoothly—or just invite them to attend, listen, and learn from those who have experienced violence firsthand because of their gender identity. Invite youth group parents and other congregational members too because learning about and praying for an end to violence against the transgender community is something about which we all need to learn.

World AIDS Day on December 1 can also be celebrated with a worship service—one that focuses on those we have lost while praying for treatment and a cure that will save humanity. In addition to worship, your youth ministry could visit or volunteer at a local HIV organization, have a frank talk about healthy sexuality, or learn from a local expert how best to be an ally to people living with HIV.

While on one end of the LGBTQ holy day spectrum, World AIDS Day and Transgender Day of Remembrance are more somber, Pride has become increasingly celebratory. In between are awareness days, days for exploration of specific communities under the LGBTQ umbrella. Bisexual Awareness Week, or BiWeek, is one such example of a visibility day that is intended to raise awareness and allow people who identify as bisexual to be proud of who they are and perhaps educate the rest of the world about the realities of being bisexual in this world. These are educational opportunities for your youth group. They will prompt discussions, dispel myths, and bring further awareness and understanding.

Appendix C at the end of this book lists many of the LGBTQ holidays and commemorative days. When observed in the context of your congregation or youth ministry, these days take on spiritual significance. Outside the walls of your church, participation in LGBTQ events is a form of both outreach and edification. As a faith leader for your youth ministry, you can bring a theological and faithful perspective to any of these commemorations and make them true holy days.

CHAPTER

10

WHAT RITUALS EXIST FOR PERSONAL LGBTQ MILESTONES?

One year, Brad and Jay found an old mirror in the storage shed at Bay Lake Camp, and they decided to incorporate the mirror into a ritual that helped youth remember their baptism at the lake. Jay stood at the edge of the water, holding the mirror while the youth approached one by one. He told the youth to look at themselves in the mirror, which they found surprisingly hard to do. He had to repeat his instruction to look at themselves, redirecting their darting eyes back to the beautiful creature that God made them to be. He then reminded them that they were created in the image of God and that, like the mirror, they reflect the beauty of God and all of God's creation. After they looked in the mirror to affirm who God made them to be, Jay directed them, one at a time, to proceed to Brad at the next "station." Brad helped them remember their baptism by dipping his hand in the lake and forming the sign of the cross on their foreheads.

We only did the mirror activity one year—for a couple of reasons. We found that when we repeated activities, youth assumed they were a tradition and that they would and should be repeated year after year. Some rituals are powerful when they are repeated annually. But sometimes rituals have an impact precisely because they aren't repeated. We decided that the mirror activity should be an example of the latter. The other more practical reason was that we couldn't find the mirror the next year!

Clearly, LGBTQ youth experience milestones that document their progress to discover more about themselves. As they bring these milestones to you, or you witness them, talk with the youth and their family about rituals that help make these milestones sacred moments.

Our creativity in worship planning both at camp and in our weekly gatherings created some new rituals (like the use of the mirror). But best of all was when the youth developed their own rituals organically. One such youth who created his own ritual—specifically a rite of passage—was John. He was bright and gregarious with a winning smile. However, he was not out to his family. This was a first for us.

After a few weeks of attending our weekly meeting, talking with friends, and much prayer and discernment, John decided he was ready to come out to his family. He was extremely nervous, but he had a really solid group of friends who were ready to support him.

John developed a ritual to bolster his support and give him the courage to come out to his family. He told us that he was throwing a "gay-la" (making sure to pronounce it just like that) at a friend's house from 5:30 to 6:00 p.m. Essentially, it was a thirty-minute party with snacks, soda, and all his supportive friends. At 6:00, he would leave the gay-la to drive home and come out to his family.

He asked if Jay and I would attend his gay-la to offer support. When we arrived, I saw about thirty teenagers in the friend's house. This was a gathering of peers. The mother of John's friend was the only other adult in the house. She was setting out snacks in the kitchen—nothing elaborate, since the half-hour gay-la was passing quickly.

John was animated and excited, flitting from person to person, getting quick hugs and words of encouragement. He had a smile on his face, but we could see the stress in his eyes. He said that his nerves weren't allowing him to stay in one place.

At 6:00 p.m., John asked if we would offer a blessing for him. His friends were of mixed faith backgrounds, and some of no faith at all, but they were all eager to participate. We gathered around John, placing our hands on his shoulders, head, and back—just as one would do for a laying on of hands in a church service. This was spontaneous: we didn't have a prepared "coming out liturgy." With no prewritten prayers, Jay and I made up the blessing on the spot. We prayed for courage, safety, and acceptance from his family. When the prayer was over, John gave all his friends one last hug, got into his car, and drove home.

John taught us about the issues of confidentiality with youth who aren't out to family members. I'll write about that part of his story later. For now, I want to focus on the gay-la and the blessing that John created for himself. The gay-la was a way to draw a supportive community together to mark a time of transition. John was uncertain about what would happen when he came out to his parents, and he was aware that he needed the support of those who knew and loved him. He asked for a blessing, for God to be present with him during the necessary task of coming out. He called on youth ministers to facilitate a prayer, and he received a physical reminder of others' support through the weight of his friends' hands on him.

John created his own informal liturgy for coming out. As youth ministers, we just followed his lead, offering blessings and support along the way. You may be approached in a similar way to offer prayer and blessing.

Any of these milestones, and whatever else the youth identify, are worthy of prayer and blessing. Like us, you could make up something on the spot. Sometimes that's what we have to do in response to a new situation. But you can also have some of these liturgies on hand for common milestones for a youth who is coming out, changing their name, updating their identity documents, finding themselves in a relationship for the first time, or accomplishing a form of advocacy.

I'm not going to provide you with LGBTQ-themed liturgies in this book, because that is not my skill. You can go on the internet to find some liturgies for name changes or coming out. However, all of these milestones are incredibly personal, so it's worthwhile to prepare something in conversation with the youth so that the blessing reflects them and their particular situation. You and they will likely find the process itself even more meaningful than the actual liturgical ritual. Who knows, if you are good enough at it, you could write a book of liturgies that the rest of us can use!

Beyond such liturgies, there are other fun ways to encourage your LGBTQ youth to take the lead and develop new traditions that help shape your youth group. Once at our summer camp, the youth had repeatedly referenced an internet meme. The meme featured a crudely designed digital banana dancing to the song "Peanut Butter Jelly Time" by the Buckwheat Boyz. The meme had reached popularity only a couple of years before, moving from online platforms to popular culture. For our coffee house talent show, one boy dressed all in yellow, put on a yellow bandanna and a pair of sunglasses, and developed a dance routine that acted out the words to the song. Like the video, his performance was a hit and was repeated over and over until it made it into the unofficial campfire songbook. And like many cultural moments, over the years, the song faded along with memory and knowledge of the original meme.

Many of these silly songs were in reference to a specific cultural phenomenon, which means they are not sacred. God did not hand down "Peanut Butter Jelly Time" to Moses along with the Ten Commandments. Jesus never preached about silly youth ministry songs. So to treat any song, whether silly or meaningful, as sacred is hypocritical. But that also means that we can develop new silly songs based on more current cultural phenomena. Oftentimes, the adults will not be sufficiently in touch with the youth zeitgeist to do this work; this initiative will come from the youth, and it takes a wise youth minister to determine when a common slang term, song, or dance move could be incorporated into an older youth ministry song or, in some cases, be developed into its own moment.

These songs and rituals had meaning within our own community, just like your songs and rituals will have meaning in your community.

CHAPTER
11

WHEN SHOULD WE BE SERIOUS AND HEAVY? WHEN SHOULD WE BE FUN AND CAMPY?

Once we brought a guest, a child development and youth ministry expert who happened to be a lesbian, to speak to the youth. She took us through an elaborate exercise in which she laid out hundreds of photographs and asked us to choose the images that most represented who we are. She was able to connect our selections to some top-line messages that reaffirmed that we were created holy and that we continue to live out our lives representing the holiness that we already are.

She was great.

But she brought a friend with her, a woman with whom we hadn't done any preplanning. This friend didn't have a sense of what The Naming Project was or what our values were. After listening to the activity and the ensuing discussion, she told us she wanted to speak to the kids too—but to give them a different kind of message.

"I think all these messages about love and acceptance aren't telling kids about how hard life is when you are LGBTQ," she said. "I want to let them know how hard it's going to be so they can be prepared for it."

I rolled my eyes. Did she really believe our youth didn't understand how difficult living in the world as an LGBTQ person was going to be? The youth had already talked about bullying. Some had talked about a lack of acceptance at home or at church. They were hearing the news about anti-LGBTQ laws being passed in states around the country. Some had seen anti-LGBTQ protestors at Pride events or elsewhere. The youth were painfully aware of how difficult life was going to be. I didn't see how an adult reminding them was going to be helpful.

We didn't let her give her talk to the youth. Instead, her colleague focused on some of the theological and historical roots of anti-LGBTQ sentiment. She also pivoted to the theological and biblical foundations that the youth could use when standing up for themselves and each other.

The tension between when to be somber and heavy and when to be fun and silly has existed in youth ministry for a long time, and it is one that we have felt acutely. At The Naming Project, we want to give youth a space to talk about what is going on in their lives without projecting our own challenges and views of the world onto them. At the same time, our youth ministry should be a place that can help us all put the worries and anxieties of the world on the back burner and recenter ourselves. That recentering sometimes involves playing games, singing silly songs, and laughing a lot.

When we were planning our first summer camp, we wanted our last night to leave a lasting emotional impact on our campers. I remembered the last night of camp when I was a child—the deep sharing, the one last goodbye, the delayed sleeping just to eke out some more time together. So we planned a final night that would bring them through all the emotional highs and lows.

We followed a high-energy and loudly affirming Coffee House Cabaret with a combined worship and campfire. This was an elaborate plan that involved movement around the entire camp and various prayer and devotion stations.

We gathered outside the chapel, and I addressed the youth: "Earlier this week, we talked about sin and confession and all those things that burden and alienate us from God, from one another, from church, and from society. Things that we struggle and wrestle with. Tonight I want you to think of something specific. Maybe a name that someone called you, an act of violence that's been done, a broken relationship, someplace where you've seen injustice in the world."

Those burdens would be represented by stones. We had found stones—not small ones but large, heavy stones. They could be carried but would take both hands and a fair amount of effort. Jay gave each camper a stone, slowly lowering it into their hands, ensuring they could feel its weight as they held it. We then led them on a walk from the indoor chapel to an outdoor chapel on the lakefront. We walked in silence, contemplating what sort of burden we were carrying in our hands. What was normally a five-minute walk felt much longer when we were carrying burdens in the darkness and silence. The moment felt as weighty as the stones in the campers' hands.

Once we reached the outdoor chapel, we sang a song, and I invited the campers to lay down their stones at the foot of a trio of crosses at the shore. I then offered absolution for the burdens they carried: "We can live as people freed from burdens if we can lay them down at the foot of the cross. God will forgive us, forgive those who have wronged us, and allow us to live as full human beings."

Cheesy? Yes, but I had them in the palm of my hand.

For the next leg of our journey, Lauren, one of the adult leaders, gave each of the campers a candle in a deep jar, lit the candles, and then led the youth down a small path through the woods. She asked them to remain silent. Every hundred feet, she instructed one camper to sit or stand alone in the woods, holding their candle, and "spend a little time alone with God." The walk was intended to be not a scary experience but a meditative one.

The campers were far enough apart that they were alone on the path, but they could see the light of the youth who were stationed before and after them. And they had their own candle to provide a source of light and warmth. And there they sat, silently, in the woods.

After about ten minutes, Brad, the pastor who had come up with the concept of an LGBTQ church camp, came along the path. He would approach a camper and beckon for that person to follow him, then another, and another.

Just as Lauren had shrunk the group by leaving one camper behind at a time, Brad was growing the group with each camper he picked up along the journey.

Brad led them out of the woods toward a blazing campfire. Meanwhile, I had sneaked back to the fire by another path, so by the time Brad and the youth arrived, I was standing by the fire with my guitar singing "Sanctuary," a song about preparing yourself to be a sanctuary of God.

And the youth bawled.

But we still weren't done. We had planned more, but the more skits and messages we added to the campfire, the further we got from that emotional and spiritual space. We tried to do a skit with the candles, but the lighter was faulty and the wind was strong, so the candles either didn't stay lit or wouldn't light in the first place. Eventually, the youth and the leaders were all laughing at us wrestling with the candles.

I could have been mad that our failed skit killed the mood, but the emotional manipulation of the youth was not the point of our worship or campfire. The campers knew they were loved, they knew they could lay down their burdens, and they knew they were a sanctuary for God. That was the message we were trying to send.

Eventually, we developed a program that alternated between high-energy, active, and loud events and more quiet and contemplative activities. This was by design—to not get stuck in any one mood for too long. Worship was often quieter, while dinner was animated. In the same way, contemplation and reflection time was followed by a game, which often involved running.

Our campfire started out very high energy, then slowing tapered into a quieter, more reflective experience. When I was a college-age camp counselor, I was told this was called the "inverted pyramid" of the campfire. The message portion of campfire still employed the standard skits, stories, and minisermons found at other camps. But some of our counselors found creative and meaningful ways to convey the message they wanted to get across to the campers. Some leaders kept things light.

Megan, a pastor and one of our beloved adult leaders, read the children's story *Peanut Butter Rhino*, in which a rhinoceros loses his peanut butter sandwich and enlists all his friends to help him find it—only to discover that it was stuck to his butt the whole time.[1] Instead of a traditional reading in which a leader would read a page and show the pictures, Megan told the story while walking around the campfire. Just as Rhino asked his friends to help him look, so Megan would turn, her butt facing the campers, exposing a paper peanut butter sandwich attached to the back of her pants. Campers would giggle, then laugh out loud as Megan circled the campfire, reading the book and acting out the searching. A story intended for toddlers took on a new meaning for teens when applied to the support network we build up around us, people who step in to lend a hand, sometimes going as far as to share their own resources for the good of our well-being.

Another year, a different adult leader, Michelle, set up a more serious activity. She scattered sticks around the campfire ring and told the story of a seeker looking for guidance from a wise old man. The old man picked up a stick from the ground and then dropped it again. He then told the seeker that life is a matter of picking up and putting down. Michelle invited the campers to approach the campfire and collect a stick while they identified what they needed to pick up. They then could name what they needed to put down as they dropped the sticks into the fire. One by one, the campers picked up sticks, naming positive habits and attitudes they wanted to adopt. Then one by one, they dropped the sticks into the fire, naming negative influences in their lives and behaviors of which they wanted to rid themselves. The activity was somber but not teary, serious but not emotional.

Even when it's not planned, youth can bring their personal struggles into a larger activity. Emotions are always just below the surface, waiting for the opportunity to surface. For us, one such worship activity was the use of the labyrinth at Bay Lake Camp. We spent a little time explaining to campers what a labyrinth was. A labyrinth is not a maze. There are no dead ends, no confusion about which way to go. There is only one path to the center and one path back to the outside. That path will turn and wind as you make your way to the center. The labyrinth is a tool for prayer, worship, reflection, and meditation. The labyrinth isn't exclusively Christian, and many religions use it as a spiritual practice. The journey to the center can represent our spiritual journey. Sometimes you will walk alongside or past someone else, and sometimes you will walk alone.

At camp, we would place objects along the path in the labyrinth: leaves, rocks, Scripture passages, candles, and so on. Youth could pick up an object to carry if it was helpful. If the object ceased to be helpful, they could set it down for others to carry. When they got to the center, we invited them to spend a moment in prayer.

As they started walking, I'd play the guitar to set a worshipful and reflective tone. Sometimes the music would simply be me jamming (in a worshipful way, I promise). Sometimes I'd bridge into one or more of the slower camp songs that we had been singing over the course of the week.

When they first entered the labyrinth, many of our youth were unaware of how powerful the experience would be. Despite our encouragement to journey slowly and intentionally, they typically entered with a skip and a smile. However, the journey along the path often brought up things that hadn't been examined or explored. As they walked, their pace became a little slower, their mood a little more somber.

By the time they reached the middle, some campers were overcome with emotion. Often they sat in the middle of the labyrinth crying. Eventually, our youth came to see the labyrinth as a set-aside time to cry. Much like we tried to make the campfire walk through the woods from the first summer emotional and heavy, our campers were starting to see the labyrinth as a place to let their hurt and pain pour out. Some of them began to be set off by the labyrinth, experiencing residual pain that lasted long after the experience was over.

After a few instances where several youth couldn't easily come out of the pain and trauma they were experiencing, we tweaked the labyrinth worship. We didn't eliminate it, but we changed the approach to keep the significance but make it more participatory, lighter, and about looking toward the future. Our explanation of the labyrinth included a discussion of how we journey together along with Christ. We also stationed a pastor in the center of the labyrinth. She was there to greet campers with a warm smile, or even a hug, and invite them to spend a little time in contemplation. After a bit, she offered them a blessing and reminded them that their journey doesn't end when they reach the middle but that they need to go back out into the world. She sent them back out the way they came in, along the winding path. When they exited, campers could gather to sing songs until the entire group had completed the journey.

The last few songs typically shifted from the heavier, contemplative topics to something more upbeat and energetic. Campers were encouraged to sing along rather than just sit with their own feelings. We don't stay at the labyrinth; we move on with the rest of our day, the rest of our lives. However, we found that if the labyrinth meditation time uncovered personal pain and trauma, it was hard to just smile and move on to the next activity for some campers.

The way we learned to end the labyrinth worship was critical. We sang a few more songs and then debriefed the experience with our youth. We had learned over the years that all of our programming, worship included, was not for manipulating campers for the sole purpose of extracting emotions.

We looked at other aspects of our weekly program to make sure we weren't traumatizing youth just for the purpose of manipulating their emotions. Another practice was the final campfire. We had offered a blessing and prayer for youth who were aging out of our program. Often this process made the tears flow. It was a natural reaction, but we found it difficult for the group to resume any sort of singing or activity once the waterworks started. Eventually, we would offer a blessing and prayer for the campers but ended the blessing with one of our silly songs that would incorporate the graduating youth's name, allowing other campers to offer tribute in a song that required some jumping and dancing.

We continued to have deeper and more meaningful moments with campers, but we made sure that they were not simply mired in their pain. Emotions are good, but they must be in service to a larger worship of God, better self-understanding as a created being of God, or the ways God calls us out into the world. If youth are feeling vulnerable or exposed by any of the activities, we adults have an obligation to debrief them properly so that they can both hold the weight of their emotions and continue to live in the world with other people and the rest of God's creation.

No matter to what youth you are ministering, there is always a tension between light and heavy, serious and silly. To make your ministry meaningful, don't manipulate youth but flow through the wide range of emotions that come from a community living their lives together.

CHAPTER

12

WHAT PART OF AN LGBTQ YOUTH'S STORY DO I NEED TO BELIEVE?

Believing what youth tell us about themselves has become a standard practice for The Naming Project. When a youth says that they are lesbian, gay, bisexual, transgender, queer, or any other sexual orientation and gender identity, we believe them and treat them accordingly. If in the future they come to us with a completely different identity, we still believe them; we simply adjust how we interact with them to match the new information. In some cases, that might mean not doing anything. In other cases, it may mean modifying names and pronouns or adjusting assumptions and expectations. The important thing is that we really listen and really believe what we are being told by the young person.

Young people are at an age when they are exploring who they are and how they are going to relate to the world around them. They might "try on" a label to see how well it fits.

I have realized that youths' self-discovery is their journey, not mine. I can't dictate who they are. As supportive adults, it's not our role to tell them who they are or how they should identify. Rather, we listen and ask clarifying questions.

We treat them in accordance with what they have told us about themselves until such time as they tell us something different.

It also means that we need to take what they say seriously.

Believing young people goes beyond just accepting them when they tell us who they are. We also need to believe their experiences. Through my work as a Naming Project director, I've heard my fair share of stories that involve violence, domestic abuse, and sexual assault. As a mandated reporter, I need to take those stories seriously and act appropriately.

It seems like a pretty simple rule, but in reality, the practice of listening and believing is quite difficult to do. Too often, adults don't believe youth. We've been through a lot. We have wisdom to share. In our minds, we can save them a lot of grief and anguish by providing warnings from our past failures. We want them to understand the world the way we see it.

The problem with this is that we tend to see, understand, and approach the world through our own experiences and perspectives, not the world that today's youth are experiencing. Beyond trusting our own experiences rather than the experiences of the youth, our feelings about them can also hinder our ability to believe what they say. Even as I'm preaching in this chapter about believing youth, I haven't always lived up to my own ideals. In some instances, I've dismissed, downplayed, and even mocked the truth that youth have told me. These are moments of which I'm not proud, and they are ones that continue to reinforce why believing young people, especially when they are talking about themselves, is so important.

One youth who participated in our camp, Tammy, was an attention seeker. She was loud. She talked a lot about herself. She was dramatic. In her first year at camp, Tammy shared that she had obsessive-compulsive disorder and that not knowing a daily schedule would give her extreme anxiety. We provided her with a printed copy of our schedule, letting her know that this was tentative and that we were using it merely as a guide—that we could change it if the situation called for it. The purpose of sharing the schedule with her was to help alleviate her anxiety. But she then used it to announce to the other campers what was happening next or to note loudly when we deviated from the printed schedule.

After enduring a lot of Tammy's grand announcements, I sort of numbed to her claims. When Tammy shared that one of her parents was transgender, I rolled my eyes and just said to myself, "There she goes again."

Years later, through social media, I saw that Tammy's parent had indeed transitioned. Tammy had been telling the truth, and I was too ignorant about transgender people and had made too many assumptions about Tammy's personality to listen to her and believe what she had been telling me.

Years later, this happened again with another youth with a similar bombastic personality. I had already determined in my head that Garrett was obnoxious and self-aggrandizing. His personality had grated on me personally, and I let that influence my interactions with him.

Another adult leader approached me to say that Garrett shared in the small group discussion that he had been sexually assaulted. We had trained our adult leaders to be mandated reporters, and they knew they needed to report any instance of harm. This counselor was doing the right thing and following procedure by bringing this news to me.

The first words out of my mouth were, "Do you think he's telling the truth?"

Not the correct first reaction!

We pulled Garrett aside to remind him that we were mandated reporters and that a sexual assault was something we would need to disclose. Garrett said he understood and provided us with more details about what had happened. We let him know that we wanted him to be safe and what the next steps would be. We then let him rejoin the group at lunch.

Once Garrett left, the other adult leader said to me, "I have to say, it's really disappointing that your first reaction to the report was not to believe Garrett." She was right, and I knew it.

Since that encounter, the news has been filled with stories of people who have been similarly dismissed. The #MeToo movement helped uncover many instances of sexual harassment and assault that had been ignored or written off over the course of years. Even after those stories came to light, people continued to question, dismiss, and mock those who had come forward.

Believing people is an interpersonal challenge. It's also a youth ministry challenge. And as our headlines proclaim, it's a societal problem. Believing what people tell us about themselves and their experiences is not just an LGBTQ issue but one that affects us all.

To bring this discussion back to our main focus, LGBTQ youth need confirmation that they and their experience of life are not just valid but valued. To believe someone is to recognize their humanity. It is to acknowledge that God created them and is still at work in their lives. It also opens us up to the possibility of seeing and experiencing God in a way we never have before. As adults, we should all be so lucky to recognize that God is working in our lives in a way we never expected.

CHAPTER
13

WHEN SHOULD I KEEP CONFIDENCE AND WHEN SHOULD I REPORT?

I t is never appropriate for an adult to disclose a youth's sexual orientation or gender identity. Not to parents. Not to other youth. Not to fellow adult leaders in your ministry team. Not even to your senior pastor.

Young people need to be in control of their stories even in the chaotic throes of adolescence. While youth are still formulating what they know about themselves, they need to be sure that their self-discoveries and stories will not get back to anyone with whom they haven't shared them yet. When we disclose someone else's identity or journey, we take away their self-determination, and we use their story to bolster our own power. We also do not know what consequences might ripple out—even from seemingly well-intentioned "outings." As youth ministry professionals, our job is to listen, advise when it's helpful, and pray. After that, the decisions and actions are up to the youth.

There is one important exception. Adult leaders should view themselves as mandated reporters who are legally required to bring suspicions of abuse or neglect of children to the authorities. In our weekly meetings in the basement of Bethany Lutheran Church, our adults are volunteers and not professionals, so we required them to disclose any such information to one of the directors, who would then join them in filing a report with the proper authorities, often something like Children and Family Services.

At the beginning of each weekly meeting, we reminded the group that anything that was shared within our community would be kept in confidence—with one important exception: if a youth shared that they were being hurt or were going to harm themselves, we would be required to report it. We reminded the youth that we wouldn't pressure them into sharing anything, but we could not keep abuse or suicidal thoughts a secret and needed to get the youth help as quickly as possible. By clearly stating the ground rules up front, youth could decide whether to share something.

We repeated this same announcement about confidentiality and mandated reporting at the beginning of each camp session. During a week away at camp, it is easier for a youth to feel comfortable enough in the community that they share something they might have kept to themselves during a two-hour meeting. Besides the announcement at the beginning of the week, we asked counselors to remind campers of the mandated reporting rule occasionally, especially in small group or one-on-one discussions.

Outside of the instances in which the mandated reporter rule applied, it was important for us to keep confidentiality. Sometimes youth told us about parents who weren't accepting, or uncomfortable, or still had a lot of questions. Stories like these are frustrating but don't legally require intervention through reporting. Nor is it usually helpful to intervene in such parent-child interactions that often simply take time to sort themselves out. Keeping confidence means we cannot intervene unless the youth asks us to or violence is occurring.

Keeping confidence was a task for the whole community, not just the leaders. And that's hard. Some youth are eager to share gossip or news or stories. We have to reinforce the idea that each person's story belongs to them. We cannot shape their story by telling others about it. This also means we cannot bring stories and personal information home from the safe space we are trying to build at camp or at weekly meetings.

Remember John, the boy who threw himself a gay-la? When he first joined us at The Naming Project, he was worried that his family would find out that he was really at a gathering for LGBTQ youth, and he took steps to cover his tracks. He would tell a friend that he wanted to come to The Naming Project so that the friend could help cover for him. He would then tell his family that he was going to the gym with his friend. This was well before phones had location trackers on them, so it was relatively easy for him to get away with it. He would spend time at The Naming Project, then change into gym clothes before returning home.

We talked for a long time about how best to support John. This was the true test of our values and principles. Were we aiding and abetting John's dishonest actions concerning his family? Were we offering courage and strength so he could come out? What obligation did we have to John, the youth who was the intended beneficiary of our ministry? What obligation did we have to his family, since one of our stated goals was that we wanted families to be able to stay together even though we knew that wasn't the case for a number of LGBTQ youth?

We didn't require John, or any of our youth, to present a parental permission slip to attend a two-hour meeting in a church. We were a group that was open to any youth who was interested in spirituality and sexuality. A few straight-identifying youth also attended. In that sense, coming to our meeting wasn't any different from going to the mall or to a restaurant. Or a gym.

Because one of our core values is confidentiality, we didn't feel any requirement to communicate with John's family. There was a credible fear that if John were outed to his family, they might reject him. We did not want to contribute to another LGBTQ youth being homeless and alienated from his family.

We discussed the matter among ourselves and even checked with our advisory board. They listened and affirmed our plan to keep allowing him to attend, keep listening to what was happening in his family, and keep being a supportive (but unobtrusive) presence in his life.

Eventually, John decided he wanted to come out to his family. He arranged the previously described gay-la to give him the courage and conviction to do so. We were there to offer support and a blessing, but the work of coming out would be his, not ours.

One week after the gay-la, we learned how John's coming out had gone. John had gone home, eaten dinner with his family, and was all set to come out. But the family was eager to watch the latest episode of *Gilmore Girls*. So John had to wait. After the show ended, he turned off the television and told them he had something to say to them.

They didn't take the news very well.

He didn't mention his involvement with The Naming Project, but they were aware that he had lied to them about his whereabouts on some occasions. He didn't meet the fate of so many youth who are kicked out of their homes, but his parents did subsequently restrict his movements and activities. He didn't return to The Naming Project after he came out to his parents, and we only heard about what had happened through some of the other youth.

John's experience was formative for affirming the limits of The Naming Project's involvement in the lives of our youth. When John was in our presence, we listened to him, we prayed for him, and we offered whatever advice seemed appropriate. However, we are not social workers or psychologists. We can't control his life or his family from our position. We had even pledged that participation in The Naming Project was confidential, meaning we weren't going to "out" him to his family. That was his decision to make, and we needed to honor his life by letting him determine his actions. After all, he would be the one who felt the repercussions.

We would only have intervened if he was being harmed. Had he been expelled from his home, we would have worked with the proper agencies to make sure his basic needs were met. Had he been abused, we would have reported that to the authorities. But John was none of those things. He was simply a teenager who was coming out to his family, and they were not supportive.

We could only see him when he came to The Naming Project or when he explicitly invited us into a moment in his life, as he did with the gay-la. It wouldn't have been appropriate for us to try to intervene in his family life. However, if he had come back to us, we would have been ready to welcome him into the group with open arms, and we would have resumed what we had been doing before: listening, advising as much as was helpful, and praying.

This has implications for all of us who work with youth. No one can erase the pain or struggle of others—not pastors, not youth ministers, not even family members. Sometimes our role is simply to be a supportive, stable presence in the midst of chaos, pain, or struggle.

Supportive pastors and youth ministers may be tempted to encourage LGBTQ youth to come out to family and friends, to live their full lives as God created them to be. After all, we assume coming out is a celebration . . . isn't it? October 11 has even been designated National Coming Out Day. It was created to recognize that no major change in politics or culture will happen if people do not realize how many LGBTQ people are in their lives. Since 1988, when National Coming Out Day was founded, the act of coming out has been treated as much less radical than it once was.

Coming out is an individual act that has collective implications. The more people come out, the more non-LGBTQ people know and understand our lives, which in turn leads them to support policies and create a culture that protects LGBTQ people, which in turn makes it safer for more LGBTQ people to come out and live their authentic lives. While coming out is good for the overall LGBTQ movement, it continues to carry personal risk for the individual. The hard reality is that family rejection and, by extension, homelessness are real, credible fears for LGBTQ youth. Nearly 40 percent of homeless youth identify as LGBTQ. And 90 percent of LGBTQ youth are homeless either because the family expelled them or because the family harassed them so badly that the youth ran away from home.[1]

Even in what can be perceived as a progressive family, youth still worry about what sort of reaction they will get. And they have good reason to worry. We continue to hear stories of youth who are rejected by their families, including one young man who recorded the incident on his phone and shared it in a viral YouTube video.[2]

There have been occasions on which I have advised youth not to come out for their own safety. To grow up to be healthy members of society, they need to stay safe. That won't happen if they are kicked out of their home, expelled from a school that requires them to sign a "lifestyle covenant" that rejects LGBTQ identity or relationships, or fired from their job—just for being honest about a part of their identity. As much as I want them to have the freedom to share their lives, their identities, and their loves with others, I realize they need to be safe before they can do that. That may happen only when they are older, when they have a college degree, or when they have moved out of their parents' home.

A youth's story is theirs alone. They need to be in control of their story—who hears it and under what circumstances. That's why we adults can be a supportive presence, can provide backup, and can encourage and advise but cannot tell their story for them. Unless there is serious harm occurring, it is not our place to step in. Our job is to allow young people to share their stories and identities as and when they choose.

CHAPTER

14

WHAT KIND OF ADULT SHOULD LEAD LGBTQ YOUTH MINISTRY?

Who makes the best kind of leader for LGBTQ youth ministry? Should it be someone who is LGBTQ? Are straight allies OK? What vetting do LGBTQ adult leaders need? What training do they need?

When we were first forming The Naming Project, one of our biggest fears was that people might view with suspicion the idea of three gay men working with youth. It's a completely false assumption, but people do conflate "gay" with "pedophile," especially given the Catholic Church clergy sex scandal of 2003. Catholic leaders decided that the problem was with gay priests, and they began a crackdown in their own seminaries, looking for candidates who had what the leaders thought was too much "gay paraphernalia."

In such a climate, we knew that any LGBTQ-affirming youth ministry had to be above reproach. We had to be prepared to respond to any accusation by having in place as comprehensive a risk-management plan and handbook of policies and procedures as possible. So for a start, all our adult leaders, including the three of us founders—Brad, Jay, and I—had to submit applications and complete background checks. We used those background checks to probe for appropriate personal information, a person's motivations for wanting to volunteer for The Naming Project, and references for character and ministry experience.

One reason for requiring an application and background check is that it kept the youth safe. We needed documentation not only from them but from an independent third-party company that performed background checks. By requiring them to submit an application and go through a background check, we created a file on our leaders. Sexual misconduct, abuse, or issues with minors would automatically disqualify someone from service.

Yet we wanted the background check to be protection for The Naming Project, not a weapon. We therefore provided a space for any applicant to explain anything the background check might turn up. Those items prompted a continued conversation with the potential volunteer. They were allowed to talk and explain what they had experienced and what they learned from their experiences. We know that people sometimes have challenging or difficult pasts and that those pasts can inform and benefit their ministry. Some of our adult leaders are social justice advocates who have marched, protested, and performed civil disobedience, which can result in a criminal record. Another may have an old, low-level offense from when they were young, perhaps closeted and figuring themselves out. Instances like these can warrant a further conversation and, if necessary, modification of duties to mitigate risk. One of our leader's background checks turned up an old drunk-driving charge. We talked to him, and the best solution was that he wouldn't be operating a vehicle during the program, which was unlikely to have happened anyway.

Such steps we took out of an abundance of caution. As an LGBTQ youth ministry, we knew we were under intense scrutiny. However, the actions we took are ones that *every* youth ministry should be undertaking, although they are often neglected in congregations with straight adult leaders. *All* your leaders need thorough training and vetting. Candidates for LGBTQ ministry leadership do not require extra scrutiny just because they are LGBTQ. And they should receive just as much training as any other adults who are working in youth ministry. The heteronormative narrative that LGBTQ people are the ones who are dangerous to children has actually left children vulnerable to abuse from straight leaders. Clergy sexual misconduct continues in *every* religious group, without respect to sexual orientation or gender identity. The only difference is how each group prevents and responds to it.

Response is key. You may receive an outpouring of responses to your idea for a ministry geared to LGBTQ youth. After *Camp Out*, a documentary film about our first summer camp, aired on television, we received emails from several adults who had watched it. And those emails continued as The Naming Project gained more media attention. The most common refrain was "I wish there had been a camp like this when I was a kid."

That sort of envy is understandable. Young people today are freer to be out and open about who they are than has been the case in the past. The adults from whom we hear are often mourning what they regard as a lost opportunity to have a faithful understanding of who they are, be accepted for it, and still have the youthfulness that our culture values so deeply. The stories about The Naming Project make them feel as if a life lived as an out LGBTQ youth passed them by.

Many of the emails we receive also included offers to volunteer at the camp, whether as a counselor, cook, or cleaner. Some of the emails come with long explanations of the writer's spiritual journey; others include a résumé of their professional accomplishments. Others simply say, "I would love to help with the camp."

When I see such emails offering help, I have a few reactions. First, I am gratified that our youth ministry is getting attention and that people are seeing it as meeting a real need. No matter what else, we can be proud of getting a response. Then I feel guilty because I know the vast majority of these potential adult volunteers won't be able to serve. Our program is small. The site we use, Bay Lake Camp, supplies its own dining, lifeguards, and support staff, so we don't need adult volunteers unless they're counselors. I think people imagine that we have hundreds of LGBTQ youth clamoring for a place at our camps. The only volunteer position we have during the camp week is counselor, and with twenty campers, seven counselors are already more than enough.

Besides, I know virtually nothing about these strangers who are emailing me. Even when they send lengthy emails detailing their faith journey and their professional accomplishments, such unsolicited emails rarely result in a job offer. As a director and youth minister, my priority is to keep the youth safe. The initial strategy for safety means working with people that I already know have a track record of excellent ministry. I'm going to trust those I know and those who come highly recommended by people I know.

If this feels exclusionary, it is. We have mitigated risk by trusting known adult leaders. Even then, all of us staffers go through an initial background check and periodic follow-ups. We exercise extreme caution.

The most obvious flaw in this system of recruiting from a pool of people we already know is that we limit who the youth get to see as role models. For them to experience a broader range of adult LGBTQ and allied folks, we need to expand the pool of counselor candidates while keeping the same stringent application, background check, and training system in place. And as we expand our pool, we want to be strategic about what adult leaders can be most helpful for the range of youth who participate. Transgender people, people of color, women, and people with disabilities are all underrepresented as leaders in the church and in The Naming Project. We need to keep this in the front of our minds as we are recruiting and vetting potential adult leaders.

We also look for people with a range of skills and knowledge. Our youngest adult must be at least five years older than the oldest youth, so we consider only people who are at least twenty-three years old. They have usually completed college and have developed a knowledge base that will be useful and necessary at camp. Some of the knowledge or skills in which we're interested are music, song leading, arts and crafts, HIV and healthy sexual education, games and recreation, activism, and nature engagement.

One of our counselors who combined just such a variety of skills is Dwaine. In terms of recruitment, Dwaine is a rare exception because he joined The Naming Project without the personal referral or previous connection on which we tend to rely. He sent us an email outlining his expertise in dance and HIV education.

Dwaine and I communicated extensively. It was only after several emails and a long phone conversation that I even sent him the application form. This has become the standard practice for all our counselors, regardless of whether they contact us or we ask them to volunteer. The form includes many basic questions about contact information and availability. But we also ask more direct questions, like how they identify, what their previous camp experience is, how they define their faith, and what skill sets they bring to camp. The application also includes consent for a background check.

After I received his completed application form, Dwaine and I had yet another conversation about how best to use his skills and background to support the ministry of The Naming Project. He is a professional dancer with a degree in kinesiology. I explained to him that our camp schedule has a gap between breakfast and Bible study, both seated activities. We needed something to fill that gap that would help the youth wake up, move, and stretch. We had been doing team-building activities such as going on trust walks, where one youth blindfolded another and led that person around the campsite. Or they would untangle themselves from a human knot. The nature of the activity reflected whoever was leading it. Sometimes it was more active, sometimes more contemplative. But it was a way to get youth outside, moving, and interacting with each other in some way.

So I tasked Dwaine with filling the time between breakfast and Bible study with some activity to get the youth moving. As a professionally trained dancer and choreographer, Dwaine took my assignment in a completely new direction, one that I came to love. During the appointed time, he met with the youth, starting the session with a yoga warm-up, getting them stretched out and limber. He then worked with them to choreograph a dance routine to a preselected song that matched our theme. Youth would rehearse every morning of camp in preparation for a performance for the Bay Lake staff and any other groups sharing the camp that week. The youth also performed it at the Coffee House Cabaret at the end of the week. It was more than I could have asked for. We called it "disco yoga." He encouraged the youth as they worked on his choreography and challenged them to push themselves further. I don't know quite how he convinced every youth to participate, but they all took the rehearsals very seriously. I walked by the room at one point and saw youth doing crunches. When I asked Dwaine why those were necessary, he explained to me that strong abs will help the youth lift each other up, while weak abs will result in the youth pulling each other down.

Dwaine was also an HIV and sexual health educator. He worked in an HIV prevention program for young queer men of color. He was quick to share that a big part of his job was to promote the empowerment of being one's self in the world without being controlled by something or someone, be that sex, drugs, alcohol, a partner, or a parent. This part of his skill set covered another area that was important to us: quality and faithful sex education for a range of sexual orientations, gender identities, and bodies. (We'll cover more in a later chapter about why that is important and how best to accomplish it.) To have found an adult leader with experience, expertise, and an unflinching willingness to take seriously every question and provide an honest and value-laden answer was invaluable.

Besides the expertise he brought to our camp, Dwaine was an energetic and flamboyant personality. Along with being a charismatic and engaging dance teacher, Dwaine was also an out and proud gay Black man who was unafraid to call out microaggressions and to remind youth and adults of the intersections between racism, sexism, homophobia, and transphobia. His skill set and personality are a great match for the camp's needs.

Yet even for those adult volunteer counselors like Dwaine who make it through the stringent application process, we still hold a training to remind them, and all of us, that the camp is for the youth, not their own experience. The activities we do—the discussion, the songs, everything—are designed to help youth explore their relationship with God and the rest of the world. Hence The Naming Project's risk-management plan states that all our leaders must put the welfare of the youth and the well-being of The Naming Project before their own wishes or personal needs. On a physical safety level, adult leaders are required to do everything possible to provide safety or rescue, right up to but stopping at the point of putting their own lives in jeopardy.

Being present for the youth also means foregoing adult-oriented activities that leave youth out. Adults who volunteer at our summer camp are on duty from the moment the first campers arrive in the Twin Cities until the last camper is dropped off. Staff members are not allowed to drink alcohol during The Naming Project camp week—neither when campers are present nor when performing duties away from camp property. Likewise, gambling is prohibited. We stagger breaks so that counselors have downtime to check in with life back home or to take a nap. Other than that, staff members are engaging with or responsible for the youth, and that responsibility includes at night when everyone is sleeping. Very occasionally, we allow an adult counselor to go off-site, but they are rare exceptions to the rule that everyone is to be at Bay Lake—or traveling to or from there—together.

Placing youth at the center of our ministry goes beyond physical safety and rules about specific behavior. It also means orienting all our actions so that youth can experience a community that is for them. It means listening to youth about *their* experiences of life rather than telling them how it is for us. It means not conflating their experiences with ours or assuming that they are seeing, hearing, and feeling the same things we do. Thus if a member of staff needs to get something off their chest, we require them to talk to one of the directors, away from the youth. Emotions are a natural way of processing the world around us. But we don't allow counselors to use the youth as their emotional crutches.

Many adult leaders find there is one youth each summer with whom they connect more than others. Maybe that youth reminds them of their younger self. Maybe that youth is facing something similar to what they've gone through. It's natural to be drawn more to one personality than the others. But there is a danger in spending too much time, attention, and energy on a single youth. It means that we are neglecting the others. It also means that we can start to project our feelings onto the youth with whom we identify. What's important to remember is that these youth are not us, and their experiences of the world are different from ours. It is our job as adults to ensure we aren't projecting ourselves onto the youth.

So what kind of adult should lead LGBTQ youth ministry? As much as possible, your adult leaders should reflect the wide range of gender identities, sexual orientations, and gender expressions. They should be role models, people from whom the youth can learn, and they should provide a diverse network of support. Your adult leaders should demonstrate passion and compassion and understand why the physical, mental, emotional, and spiritual safety of LGBTQ youth is paramount. They should be willing to undergo a thorough and rigorous application process to ensure the safety of the youth and compatibility with the needs of the camp. They should be trained and equipped in the policies and procedures as well as the best practices for ministry with LGBTQ youth. And they should be prepared to bring their full range of talents to share with the youth to whom they will be ministering.

CHAPTER

15

WHAT RELATIONSHIP
GUIDELINES CAN THE CHURCH
TEACH LGBTQ YOUTH?

When we started The Naming Project in 2003, we maintained a strict "no photograph" policy when it came to our youth. Our first printed brochures featured the backs of youth, never showing their faces. In retrospect, it looked very much like an "LGBTQ Youth Anonymous" group, which was the intention at the time. We assumed, rightly or wrongly, that youth wouldn't want to be publicly identified and outed through our materials.

This policy held until we started the summer camp program, which presented its own challenges. Before our first camp, a film producer approached us, wanting to make a documentary about our camp. This meant that our youth, who heretofore had been anonymous, were now going to be very public. We decided that we would provide an opt-in policy for photos and videos. As a part of our registration process, we included a photo and video waiver. This was separate from the participation waiver that they signed. It required the signature of both the parent and the youth. But it also was completely optional. We just had to know who hadn't signed the form and not include them in photographs. If we accidentally included them in a photo or video, we had to either crop them out or not use the image at all.

Signing a release form weeks or months before the start of camp isn't the same thing as wanting an image of you in each and every situation to be made public. We made the film crew agree that at any moment, the youth had the option to say they didn't want to be filmed and that the film crew would respect their wishes.

Among the group, besides themselves, the youth were not aware of who had signed the release or not. Only we leaders (and the film crew) knew. We needed to implement a continued practice of asking about photos and giving people ample opportunity to opt in or opt out. So in addition to the waivers being included in our registration, we encouraged the practice of asking permission before photos were taken, especially of individuals.

But there was still the matter of youth taking each other's photos. When we first established our policy, we assumed that youth would take photos on a handheld camera and keep all relevant photos for themselves or perhaps exchange printed copies with one another. We didn't anticipate the advent of social media platforms on which youth would be posting, sharing, and tagging photos of their fellow youth in the wider world. We didn't realize that cameras would be integrated into the cell phones that everyone carried with them at all times and that were connected to the web, making posting and sharing easier than ever.

After a few years of grappling with how to create a rule that both was fair and ensured youths' protection from unwanted social media attention, Logan finally educated the rest of us about the "culture of consent." What began around discussions of photos on social media platforms soon expanded helpfully to a wide array of behaviors.

The "culture of consent" refers to asking for permission rather than assuming that permission is given. As it relates to photography, it meant that all of us, youth and adult leaders alike, needed to obtain advance permission to take and share any photos in our community. It could be a blanket permission (like the written permission for which we asked in the registration form), or it could be on a case-by-case basis. Again, camp participants could withdraw or give their consent at any time. The blanket permission was an indication of general willingness but was not something that meant we could take photos whenever, wherever, and of whomever we wanted.

Photography was our entry into consent culture, perhaps because it was something that was fairly concrete and understandable to our community. There were certainly much more high-stakes instances of consent that we had to address. The next phase of our discussion around consent culture was about hugs.

Logan led the charge in helping make consent culture go beyond photography and hugs, as a way to understand all our relationships, whether friendship, romantic, or sexual. Logan was educated in the faith-based Our Whole Lives[1] sexuality curriculum, developed by the United Church of Christ and Unitarian Universalist Association, which took "consent culture" from a concept to be discussed to a way to help youth think through why consent is important and what the challenges are of signaling and understanding consent.

We started our time together with the rules around photographs, then talked about hugs. Logan then introduced consent culture to the youth. Instead of starting with hugs, Logan led us through a much more low-stakes activity: they asked us to find a partner and to think of five different ways to ask for a high five. Each person's partner had to find five creative ways to say yes and five ways to say no. The practice was to remind us of what we should be asking when we want to initiate touch. It also let us practice various ways to communicate a yes and a no.

Our community, like many church communities, can be a pretty huggy community. As adult leaders, we were aware of the power dynamic that existed in our hug giving, and we had to be very careful. During our adult training sessions, we stressed that adult leaders are expected to give equal attention to all youth, to conduct themselves with the highest propriety and respect for others, and to put no one in an intimidating, uncomfortable, or threatening situation. We can hug, but we should always be aware of when our hugs are too long or too tight. Our hugs must be distributed and not focused on one youth. A-frame hugs, with the shoulders touching but the hips and feet at a distance, and side hugs, with arms over each other's shoulders, were helpful to make sure that there wasn't inappropriate touching. We reminded the adult leaders that if a recipient interprets a hug as inappropriate, then it *is* inappropriate.

We needed a way to communicate our policy to the youth that identified sexual harassment not just as a rule to avoid breaking (though it certainly was a rule) but as a way to value each other as beings created in the image of God. We needed to dispel the myth that hugs were mandatory or even culturally expected within our community. We also wanted to let youth know that touch could certainly be comforting and powerful and not just inappropriate and sexual. Talking explicitly about consent culture is a way we communicate this nuance to young people. It's a helpful practice that churches can replicate easily with their young people.

Some of our youth really wanted and appreciated hugs. We made an announcement at the orientation about people's different feelings about hugging and touching. One girl proclaimed to the group, "I love hugs, so you can hug me." The announcement set the tone that she would be a hugger, and it let everyone know she welcomed hugs. But she wasn't asking herself whether everyone else liked hugs as much as she did. Very few youth are bold enough to make an announcement in front of a group that they *don't* want hugs.

Those youth who are comfortable with hugs are often unaware that touch can be interpreted in many different ways—for example, that it can overstimulate a person or be perceived as sexualized touch.

The line between innocent hugging and sexual harassment is going to be different for each person. We have a sexual harassment policy in our risk-management plan that defines sexual harassment as any verbal, written, or physical sexual advance, suggestion, or conduct that is unwelcome or conduct that creates an offensive, hostile, or intimidating environment. If an adult leader witnessed such behavior or if it was reported, we would take it seriously. Anyone present should intervene immediately in such a situation and if needed include another director in the intervention.

Later in that first week of camp, Logan facilitated a longer conversation about consent culture. That consent culture conversation gave us an entry into a larger conversation about relationships and sex education. Consent isn't only about sex, although consent is essential to any romantic or sexual relationship. Consent is also about your relationships with your friends, coworkers, and fellow church members and the strangers you meet on the street. Consent is about honoring and respecting God's creation and the discovery process that we all go through to figure out who we are, what we like, and what sorts of relationships we want to form.

The human race has repeatedly violated consent and imposed control when it comes to relationships, and Christianity has not been exempt from that history. The dowry system facilitated the sale of daughters into marriage in return for money, animals, or objects of value. The system treated women as property, with no control over their relationships or their bodies. Leviticus even provides a mechanism by which to resolve a dispute between a groom and the father of the bride about whether the bride was a virgin. Today, the modern purity movement exerts strict control over girls and their bodies. All that history has culminated in a culture that ignores and minimizes sexual assault while also pressuring teens into sexual behavior before they are ready.

In the next chapter, I'll talk about faithful LGBTQ sex education, but we found that, for us, it had to start with an acknowledgment that God created us with care and love. We have autonomy over our bodies because they are the bodies that God gave to us. God formed us to be in relationships that are life giving both to us and to others. Setting and keeping boundaries and consent are essential for healthy relationships of any sort.

Logan asked the youth, "What makes for a good friendship?" The youth responded with several ideas: trust, open communication, safety, respect, shared interests, equality, and sense of humor. Others offered responsibility, understanding, support during good and bad times, self-esteem, availability, reciprocity, and growth.

Logan then asked, "What makes for an unhealthy friendship?" The responses came back even more forcefully: lack of time, violence and fighting, disrespect, misunderstanding, and breaking trust.

Logan asked the same sorts of questions about romantic relationships, urging the youth to think about the connection between friendships and relationships. Is it different from what makes for a good friendship? What are big signs that a relationship, either romantic or simply friendly, is unhealthy or possibly dangerous?

Logan then addressed boundaries. Setting boundaries is an exercise in knowing ourselves, what we want, and for what we are ready. Examples of boundaries include things like alone time, phone privacy, speaking to each other respectfully, never calling each other names, and outing someone against their will. Logan ended by sharing a working definition: "Boundaries are the distance from which I can love both you and me at the same time."

Logan then threw a discussion question back to the youth: "What's a good reason to break up?" After much discussion, the group landed on the reality that simply wanting to break up is enough reason to do so. No one should be forced to stay in a relationship that isn't life giving, as it was intended to be.

We then ended the first part of our conversation on relationships and consent with a game of "Healthy or Unhealthy." Logan read first-person statements like "I insist on knowing where my romantic partner is when we aren't together." We then engaged in a debate around the statement, the behavior behind each statement, and what circumstances would make such a statement healthy or unhealthy.

The activity helped the youth think through all the ways that consent could be expressed or denied. Such bridging between the community we were building and the "real world" can help the youth think critically about other aspects of their life, examine their actions, and look for ways in which they can assert their own boundaries with others. It also helps set the tone for how we can talk about sex from a faith perspective and inclusive of LGBTQ bodies and relationships the next day . . . and in the next chapter.

16

WHAT IS FAITHFUL LGBTQ SEX EDUCATION?

"**D**o you guys ever get frustrated?" Cameron asked. "Like, sometimes, I'm in my room by myself, and I'm feeling so . . . frustrated, and I don't know what to do."

We were just about to wrap up our small group discussion on sex and sexuality. Youth had chosen to attend one of three different groups based on their gender identity. Cameron's repeated use of the word *frustrated* made me arch my eyebrows, but before I could say anything, another boy spoke up.

"Maybe you need something to do with your hands . . . like learn to play the guitar." The other boys all quickly agreed. Cameron thanked them for their input, and the group dispersed for lunch.

Adult leader Greg gave me a look that said, "We need to debrief this." After the others were gone, I said, "Do you think he really meant . . ." but before I could finish the sentence, Greg said, "Oh yeah, someone needs to talk to him. There is no way he was talking about playing the guitar."

I said I would talk to him and spent the rest of the day looking for an opportunity to revisit the topic with Cameron. Later, during the afternoon free time, I approached Cameron. "How was the advice you got this morning?" I asked.

"It was really great," Cameron replied. "Those guys are so helpful. I think the suggestion to play guitar is a really good one."

"But did that answer what you were really talking about?" I prodded. "Sometimes 'frustrated' means something else."

"What does it mean?" Cameron asked, putting me on the spot. Clearly, he wasn't going to make this easy for me, and my own embarrassment about talking about sex, especially with a teenager, was causing me to be much less direct and much more awkward than I intended. It was time just to rip off the Band-Aid.

"Often, when people say 'frustrated,' they are talking about the need for masturbation," I blurted out.

Cameron looked at me for a second, and then said, "I didn't mean that at all."

The tip of my ears burned. I quickly blurted out, "Oh, OK. Then I'm glad you got good advice," and let him join his friends at the waterfront.

In my attempt to provide a listening ear and wise advice, I had further stigmatized honest conversations about sex, sexuality, and pleasure, and I had done it in a way that made me sound like the creepy adult I wanted our campers to avoid. Cameron never brought up the concern again in front of me, but to this day, I continue to wonder if he was as embarrassed as I was at the whole exchange.

Our culture reinforces a commonly held assumption that teenagers, regardless of sexual orientation and gender identity, are sex machines that will use any opportunity to fornicate. Our culture also provides messages that reinforce that youth should be having sex and that they are missing out if they aren't.

But while youth are awash in sexual images and messages, they aren't getting a lot of useful information for healthy sex and sexuality. Sex education that includes LGBTQ relationships and gender-nonconforming bodies is even rarer. Moreover, LGBTQ people face additional accusations that they are "sexualizing" matters when the realities of their relationships are discussed.

We often start the sex and relationship session with an informal poll. Only a few youth at The Naming Project had been taught comprehensive sex education in school or by their families. Some had learned about heterosexual sex and cisgender bodies but still had to figure out what that meant for their bodies and the relationships they hoped to form one day. Many of our youth had no information outside of what they saw in media or on the internet, and both of these often provided an incomplete view of the mechanics of sex, portrayed unhealthy relationship dynamics, and gave unrealistic expectations of a sexual experience. Some youth were sexually active, while others had no experience. There were even youth who felt shame because of their experience with sex or lack thereof.

As youth ministers, we want our youth to have a healthy understanding of their bodies and the choices they will have before them, but we cannot assume they are getting quality, faithful sex education anywhere else. This presents us with an opportunity.

We can assume that some of our youth are sexually active, but activity doesn't mean the same thing as being informed—as having conversations about values, choices, and safety, for example. And in this sea of misinformation, the messages about healthy sexuality and relationships from the most trusted sources—namely, family and church—often come in the form of confused or awkward silence. Some youth assume that we will judge them for their sexual activity given past messages from the church on sexuality, especially LGBTQ sexuality.

At The Naming Project, we stress that there is to be no sexual activity during our programming, including at camp. We make it clear that this is done for the good of the community. We say explicitly that we are not going to condemn their sexual activity in life, but neither are we going to allow others to feel shame for their lack of sexual experience.

We start out by letting youth know that adult leaders are open to answering their questions about sex and sexuality. But we take care to do it in a way that doesn't further stigmatize or trivialize frank discussions about sexuality. That also means that we, as leaders, should take special care not to engage in the same stigmatizing rhetoric that we so often hear.

It's easier to write about this than to do it in practice! Once, when we were meeting in small groups, Greg said, "This is also a time if you have any questions about . . . sex." The word *sex* he said in a half whisper, as if it were a dirty secret. We realized later that the way we had started the discussion conveyed the message that we were embarrassed or ashamed. Unsurprisingly, campers didn't take us up on the opportunity to ask such questions.

Other adult leaders have the background and skill to address sex and sexuality in a frank and appropriate way. Two of our leaders, Logan and Dwaine, made a very good team when talking about sex and sexuality. Both leaders rooted sex discussion in being created in the image of God, helping the campers understand that being made in the image of God means they have autonomy over their bodies and should be able to say yes or no to whatever is going to happen with their bodies. Logan used their training for Our Whole Lives to take campers through the overarching themes and values related to relationships, sex, and sexuality and found brilliant ways to tie their discussion to the biblical theme of the week.

Dwaine had a background in HIV education, and we gave him a block of time to talk about safety, HIV, and STDs. He stressed that the only completely effective form of safe sex is abstinence but also spoke to campers about various forms of protection, including providing all the relevant information about condoms and the HIV prevention drug commonly known as PrEP (pre-exposure prophylaxis). Once, he stood in front of the campers and explained, "There are different forms of lube: water-based, silicone-based, and flavored lube." He said "flavored" with an eye roll, declaring, "Do you know what you do with flavored lube? Throw it in the trash!" He went on to explain that the flavoring is mostly just sugar, which makes the lube less effective. "Have you ever seen rock candy? Well, when sugar lube dries up, it crystalizes. And you don't need that on or in your body."

While Dwaine was happy to explain or answer any "logistical" or "technical" questions about sex, he also encouraged campers to be creative and not just assume that sex or sexuality is what they'd seen in the media. For example, he said, "You may not like or want to do penetration. That is perfectly OK. You can do so many other things besides penetration. Cuddling, kissing, caressing are all great ways to be sexual without having to penetrate."

We don't want sex education to be sensational, the way that it is often portrayed in popular culture. Neither do we want to communicate that sex is bad. God gave us sex as a gift, and it should be a gift that we can enjoy responsibly. We want to counter the confusion and mixed messages that flow through our American and Christian cultures with values and useful information.

We can't always anticipate what youth have heard from outside sources or what they have been pressured into doing. We try as much as possible to be open to any questions they have and to be nonjudgmental. Often, after Dwaine had talked to the youth about sex, they would approach him individually with specific questions. Typically, they raised topics they had heard about from friends, magazines, or the internet or things they had experienced themselves. Dwaine was patient, listening to their questions and providing the answer that was most in alignment with our values of safety and faith. If youth had done something they had later regretted, Dwaine was there to provide words of comfort and affirmation and help them figure out what they could learn from the experience.

We also set out a jar into which youth could drop written questions anonymously. From time to time, we looked at the questions in the "sex jar" and found ways to incorporate answers to those questions in whole-group programming so that everyone could learn from the questions of their peers.

One important aspect of any faithful LGBTQ "sex talk" is not to separate it from discussions of health and relationships, because all of these are ultimately about faith and values. During our discussions with youth, we reiterate the qualities of healthy relationships. We help the youth discuss what red flags to look for in unhealthy relationships—as I discussed in the previous chapter. We stress the importance of consent in every relationship, sexual or not—again, as discussed in chapter 15. These are all a part of any frank and honest discussion of LGBTQ sexuality.

Even beyond relationships, sexuality also involves liking yourself and your own body. Here, Greg's background as a dietitian who has studied eating disorders in LGBTQ youth has been particularly useful. His work makes him attuned to the comments youth make about themselves and their bodies. He stresses to all of us the diversity of bodies present in God's creation, especially those represented in the LGBTQ community. He reminds us that no matter what sort of body we have, our focus on health for ourselves and the good of our bodies and spirits is paramount.

Greg often comments, "In order to be in a healthy relationship with others, you have to have a healthy relationship with yourself." When a camper says something like, "No one would want to date me anyway," Greg approaches them individually to probe what makes them feel that way. He knows that without proper self-respect, youth get pressured into relationships that violate their values and put the youth at risk. If they don't feel worthy, they don't think they are worth making wise choices about their bodies, which can include poor eating habits, lack of exercise, self-harm, or risky sexual behavior.

This same understanding manifested itself in other aspects of our program. For example, in leading youth through a yoga routine, Greg frequently reminds them that every body is different. He is careful to separate the words "every" and "body" to make each youth focus on their own body—what it is capable of, what stretches it, and what its limits are. It is more important for youth to focus on what their bodies are telling them than to follow to the letter the instructions he gives them about yoga poses.

What do yoga and healthy body image have to do with sex and sexuality? What we are really talking about here is health. Greg often says to our youth, "Whether it's physical or medical, it's *your* body that God gave you, not your parents', not your pastor's, not your doctor's, not your significant other's, and not mine. It's important that anyone who you talk to about your body—what's happening with it and how to keep it healthy—understands you and your body . . . and that takes trust." We want the list of trusted adults to include parents, pastors, youth ministers, doctors, and clinicians.

I realize that this chapter might be overwhelming. You may not know the "ins and outs" of LGBTQ sexual health. That's OK. You don't have to know everything. What you should know are the values of safety, consent, respect . . .

the same values you likely established for your whole youth group, not just its LGBTQ members. And then you should be willing to listen and, without judgment, help youth find the answers to their questions. This might mean having a listing of local HIV educational organizations, medical experts, and sex educators ready to help you answer *your own* questions without judgment.

Though each body and each relationship are different, our individual health is actually about the collective good. Perhaps LGBTQ youth can teach straight youth (and adults) what healthy boundaries are, why consent is so important, and ways to be creative with sexuality that don't have to focus on the penetrative sex that the media shows us constantly. You can combat misinformation, and you can direct youth to reliable resources to help answer their questions. And you can remind youth of the values of your community, particularly that God has created them in a wide range of diversity, which is to be both celebrated and taken seriously. *That* is faithful sex education.

CHAPTER
17

WHEN IS IT IMPORTANT TO KNOW A PERSON'S GENDER? WHY WOULD IT BE NECESSARY?

I t seems that youth ministry people often want a lot of information, especially on registration forms. On The Naming Project summer camp registration form, we ask for a mailing address, school grade completed by the time camp starts, T-shirt size, and multiple phone numbers and email addresses for both the campers and the parents. We have three blanks for parents' (including stepparents') emergency contact information (if there is an emergency, we want to get hold of someone as quickly as possible).

That's a lot of information! But there are also things for which we deliberately don't ask.

We don't ask our youth their sexual orientation. For the purposes of our ministry, a precise labeling of sexual orientation doesn't matter. We would rather hear them describe themselves organically, without needing to check a box or choose a single word that is supposed to encapsulate whom they like to be around, whom they want to date, or what kind of people they find attractive. That means listening to how they describe or talk about themselves, not asking them for a one-word answer on a form.

Most registration systems are based on checkboxes, and boxes often reduce people's identity to a single label. While labels can be a helpful shortcut to understanding who people are and grouping them appropriately, for some LGBTQ people, labels are limiting. Typically, LGBTQ youth find that a single word doesn't fully describe or encapsulate who people are. Labels leave out valuable information by ignoring the ways in which someone does not reflect the commonly held definition of whatever the label says.

We *do* ask about gender on the registration form. The challenge is how to do that in a way that doesn't entail making a choice among a limited set of options. How might we ask about someone's gender identity in a way that is empowering and not limiting? We cannot possibly list every permutation of gender identity on a form and still encapsulate the splendid diversity of God's creation.

We house youth roughly by gender, taking several factors into consideration. Some youth, including transgender, nonbinary, and gender-nonconforming youth, may experience discomfort or even trauma by being housed with people who don't share their gender identity. That is why we think gender is an important item to include on the registration form. But instead of using a checkbox on the form, we include a blank for gender, like this:

Gender: _____

This invites the camper to use their own words to describe their own identity as fully and completely as they wish. Instead of giving them a limited set of options, which are likely not to be exhaustive or to be mutually exclusive, we invite them to describe themselves briefly. In our heads, this is a great solution, given that it doesn't confine our campers to a literal "box."

We don't even explicitly ask if campers are transgender on the registration form, but we invite that information to be included on the gender blank if they want to include it. This is not a perfect solution, and consequently, it has been the subject of ongoing debate. On the one hand, whether or not a camper is transgender ultimately isn't our business. We don't intend their experience at our camp to differ from that at other camps based on their gender identity. On the other hand, if there is a way that we can be helpful to a transgender camper, we should be prepared to be so.

We found that one drawback to our approach was that parents are usually the ones who fill out registration forms, and parents don't always understand the blank. When there is no structure, people assume a structure. The years of dealing with checkboxes and legal forms have instilled in today's parents the misconception that they must fill out the registration form as if it were a legal deposition.

Some parents feel they are required to write the sex listed on their child's birth certificate. For cisgender youth, this works fine. However, if their child is transgender, parents sometimes write "born male but living as a girl" or "biologically female but living as a boy." These descriptions, while giving us an idea of who the youth is, mainly reflect that the parent is still trying to understand their child. We try to be somewhat forgiving of parents who may still be on a learning curve while interpreting the registration form to get the best sense of the youth who is going to be joining us.

If you have a transgender teen in your youth ministry—especially one who has been in the congregation or among the youth ministry for a while—you likely know them well enough to know who they are. Where you might feel less certain is when you receive a registration form for a youth with whom you don't have a previous relationship. This is the case the first time a youth joins us for camp, but it gets much easier once we know them. In the meantime, we do the best we can with the information given to us.

Sometimes this information has major deficiencies. Some parents completely neglect to tell us that their child is transgender. One year, a youth arrived fully presenting as a girl—and then showed me her registration form that still had "Victor" on it. When I asked if Victor was what she wanted to be called, she quickly said no and that she wanted us to call her Miranda.

We continue to use the gender blank on our forms and allow youth and parents to fill it out as they see fit. There are a few practical implications of this practice. First, as youth ministers, we need to interpret what is written on the blank with an open heart and open mind, looking for instances where parents may not be providing the fullest, most nuanced information. Second, it means that we must be prepared to listen to the camper directly and be prepared to adjust our plans based on what they tell us.

Keep in mind that LGBTQ people do not believe that their sexual orientation or gender identity is their exhaustive identity as a person—as is true of other people too. Sexual orientation and gender identity have always been only two of the many aspects of us but parts that engage with the rest of our identity. For those of us LGBTQ people who also identify as Christian, we believe that the source of our identity is God. We believe that God created us with our whole identity and set us in a world in which that identity is played out relationally with the rest of the world.

Anti-LGBTQ activists have made a similar, if convoluted, argument. They often discourage LGBTQ people from claiming and using language to identify themselves as a part of the LGBTQ community, calling that "labeling." The reasoning, from the anti-LGBTQ perspective, has been that accepting the label of "lesbian," "gay," "bisexual," "transgender," or "queer" somehow erases the rest of someone's identity. According to them, sexual orientation doesn't make your entire identity. Your identity isn't derived solely from sexual orientation; you are a whole, multifaceted person, not just a sex act.

The LGBTQ community knows this.

In fact, for much of their lives, many LGBTQ people would prefer that their sexual orientation or gender identity was not the sole focus for how society treats them. Whereas LGBTQ people are less focused on sexual orientation or gender identity in their everyday lives, the anti-LGBTQ industry continues to put undue attention on what is only a part of what makes us who we are.

Please also keep in mind that youth may not have the language to sum up their sexual orientation or gender identity easily. And if the youth themselves don't, then their parents filling out registrations forms may have even less language and clear information with which to work.

In conclusion, to decide whether and when you might need to know a youth's gender, ask yourself, What purpose does knowing this information serve? How will it help me minister to them more effectively? Am I grouping the youth with others to be helpful to them or to reinforce my own concept of sex and gender? Why might you want to know about a person's gender? Maybe so that you can learn more about the youth as a whole person. You may find that having less written information on a registration form opens up the channels of communication to learn even more about a young person's journey to self-understanding.

CHAPTER

18

WHAT ABOUT
SLEEPING ARRANGEMENTS?

We are *finally* getting to the question you've probably been wondering about since the beginning. Maybe it was even the question
that prompted you to buy this book: "What should I do about
housing and sleeping arrangements?" Or from a parent to you: "What will the
sleeping arrangements be?" In whatever form, it's the most common question
we're asked at The Naming Project. Some questioners explain, "At traditional
camps, you want to keep the boys out of the girls' cabin and the girls out of
the boys' cabin . . . so . . . what happens here?" These are all good questions.

It's worth asking what the assumptions are behind such questions. One
of them is that LGBTQ youth, just like all other teenagers, are horny beasts,
seeking out any opportunity to fornicate. I have covered a few ways to address
this already—namely, by stating rules that apply to the whole group (e.g., don't
have sex during church activities) and having healthy and ethical sexual health
conversations in which you address their thoughts and concerns, spoken or
unspoken.

However, there is so much more at stake in such questions than keeping teenagers from hooking up with each other at church camp. Outside of the legitimate but knee-jerk questions about "hanky-panky" are additional concerns about privacy, body image, consent, and community. At The Naming Project, it is these broader concerns that have shaped our decisions about sleeping arrangements.

For many teens, a summer camp is the first place where they share living space with peers who are not their family. Privacy is not expected. Campers live in intentionally close quarters with cabinmates, often people they don't know. They do their daily functions, like brushing teeth and sleeping, in the company of others. Their possessions are either on display or barely hidden in a suitcase sitting out in the open or shoved under their bunk.

For many of us, being placed in a cabin with strangers is the most anxiety-producing part of summer camp. When I was a child, I was excited for camp but anxious about my cabinmates. Would they be cruel and play pranks on me while I slept? Would they make fun of me for my clothing? Would they harass me for being too skinny? Would they rifle through my luggage and hang up my underwear for everyone to see? The fact that I would be attending *church* camp didn't allay my concerns: I knew kids can be cruel no matter the environment.

Obviously, no camp leaders want this behavior to happen, but they cannot completely control how campers will act. For already vulnerable persons, like LGBTQ youth, the sense of being different in some way makes them feel that much more exposed, open to ridicule, and hence anxious.

When we were planning the first Naming Project camp, we kept in mind those memories of how we had felt exposed as campers, and we wanted to make sure that we could mitigate that as much as possible for our youth. We didn't do it perfectly. We were dealing with the logistical setup of the campsite we were using. We were also more conscious of "gay and lesbian" concerns and less about other sexual orientations and gender identities. Even we were still caught up in the binary understanding of sexual orientation and gender identity.

For our first several years, Bay Lake Camp definitely had "old-fashioned" sleeping arrangements. The camp was built in 1926, when the world thought and said little about LGBTQ people and their desire to be a part of a church camp. The cabins were small wooden structures with four or five creaky metal bunk beds each. The campsite we were using was a very "gendered" space, meaning the cabins were designed for single-sex use. There was a single bathhouse for everyone on the island to shower, use a sink with running water, and have access to a toilet. The bathhouse had one side for the girls and the other side for the boys.

Given such arrangements, early on in planning our summer camp, we wondered what the best way would be to house campers who might be uncomfortable sharing a space with campers of a different gender, with campers of the same gender, and with those who were still figuring out their gender identity. In my experience, LGBTQ youth are, on the whole, incredibly modest. They are still in puberty, so their bodies are awkward and changing. The youth aren't keen on showing off and are probably more concerned about people seeing them. We concluded that everyone would want some privacy.

Who our adult counselors were also informed our decision about housing. We had four adults—three gay men and a bisexual woman. For accountability purposes, we decided that no adult would be housed alone with campers. This meant that our one female counselor couldn't be placed in a cabin by herself with the female-identified campers.

Given all these factors, we decided that for our first year, the best option was for everyone to sleep together in one big room. When the campers arrived, we told them to go into the cabins, take the mattresses off the beds, and bring them into the chapel.

At first, the campers complained. One grumbled that moving mattresses was more complicated than just staying in separate cabins. They wanted the sense of "their space" that bunk beds would offer. When everyone's belongings are out in the open on the floor, no one has privacy.

However, after some initial grumbling, the campers appreciated all staying in a room together. Not only did nights feel something like a slumber party; there was also the convenience of not having to move to a different space for Bible study and worship. It also came in handy one night when the temperature dipped into the low thirties and everyone cozied up by the fireplace together.

Our camp housing arrangements evolved after that first year, though not only as a result of our own decisions. Bay Lake Camp was undergoing a capital campaign to upgrade its buildings. In the following years, we heard the sounds of chainsaws felling trees, the existing dining hall being remodeled, cabins being made more accessible, and eventually the construction of a new lodge.

While all that construction was taking place, we used the cabins rather than the chapel for sleeping accommodations, grouping youth by the gender they expressed on the registration form. Beginning the second year, we always had at least one transgender youth, and we placed them with youth of the same gender, as expressed on the registration form or verbally by the youth, if parents didn't quite "get it" yet.

After Bay Lake Camp completed its capital plan, we were able to use the newly built lodge. It was the first winterized building of the camp. It had a large main room, two fireside lounges, and twelve bedrooms. Each bedroom had six or eight bunk beds. But the best part was that each bedroom also had two sinks, a private bathroom with a toilet and shower, and air-conditioning.

For us, this was a game changer.

We continued to group campers roughly by stated gender identity but were able to apply more nuance.

As camp went on, the number of transgender, genderqueer, and youth still figuring themselves out attending our camp continued to climb. We remained flexible but generally placed youth who shared a gender identity in a room together, including transgender campers. When we thought it was helpful, we placed younger transgender campers with ones who were older and returning to camp. That way the older campers, whom we already knew and trusted, could serve as affirming role models.

If there weren't enough campers who shared a gender identity to warrant a room of their own, we would include some of our known, mature, and welcoming campers. In many instances, the most mature camper identified as transgender, allowing them to be a leader for all the other campers with whom they shared a room.

We assigned four to six campers per room but didn't put any counselors in the rooms with the campers. Instead, the counselors usually took two rooms between the campers' rooms. We also required that all bedroom doors remain open, keeping our sleeping spaces semipublic and therefore, we hoped, safer.

Having the showers and toilets in each bedroom allowed youth to have complete privacy at some of their most personal moments. And our open-door sleeping and daytime policy maintained accountability for the community. Mixing genders and ages in shared spaces, including the adult counselors, discouraged two or more campers from separating themselves from the community for mischief. It reoriented their energy and attention to the full group rather than to their one "special someone."

In our camp rules, we reiterated that bunks are a personal space. There are multiple responsibilities in this reminder. One is for the bed occupant to keep their personal space tidy and appropriately confined. The second is to remind everyone to respect each other's space, not to rummage through another's personal possessions, and to get permission before even sitting on another person's bed. Under no circumstances would we allow campers to sleep in the same bed.

In addition to the showers and toilets in each bedroom, the lodge also had two public restrooms. They were accessible, single-stall restrooms with sinks. We encouraged Bay Lake Camp to make every single-stall restroom gender neutral.

The way we used the lodge encouraged a tight-knit community but allowed for extra privacy when and where it was needed. It was certainly not a perfect solution, but it kept us moving toward an ideal.

Recall that at the beginning of this book, I encouraged you to approach logistical questions by recalling your church's or group's core values. Housing and sleeping arrangements are precisely the kinds of logistical questions that need to be answered according to one's values. A uniform, unchanging *policy* on sleeping arrangements isn't going to help you in every environment, but a clear set of *values* will help you approach every environment with a way to solve the logistical challenges before you.

You've probably been to a camp, church, or someplace similar that assumes that everyone is heterosexual and cisgender. Camp cabins, hotel rooms, dormitories, church basements, and showers and locker rooms are all spaces used for youth ministry trips. As inclusive youth ministers, we are trying to create an inclusive program in a world that isn't ordered inclusively. Our values of inclusiveness and safety can easily run up against an architectural design or layout that perpetuates the understanding that all boys are the same, all girls are the same, and grouping boys and girls separately is optimal for everyone in those groups.

Take, for example, a youth trip that involves staying in hotels. Housing each youth in their own room ensures privacy . . . but is prohibitively expensive. Two in a room allows each youth to have their own bed but has them still sharing a sleeping space. To minimize the per-person cost, many youth groups place four youth to a room, requiring them to share beds or sleep on the floor. In many small churches, there may be one LGBTQ youth in the mix, and the question is where to place that child.

In addition to the range of housing types you'll encounter, your youth group will also likely be constituted of an ever-changing mix of sexual orientations and gender identities. Some camps promote a "genderqueer" housing option for campers who don't fit into the gender binary. That approach can work as long as you have a critical mass of youth to house in the genderqueer space. Housing a single transgender camper in a room or cabin by themselves is isolating and stigmatizing. It sends the message that they aren't safe around anyone else and that others aren't safe around them.

If your values include safety, then think of the options that are going to keep *everyone* safe, physically, mentally, and emotionally. Instead of, for example, viewing a transgender teenager as the challenge to the way we've organized youth in the past, think of ways to keep the transgender teen as well as their peers safe and comfortable. For a retreat or lock-in, that may mean sharing one large room like we did our first year of camp. In a hotel situation, that isn't possible. Placing a transgender teen in a room with peers they don't know, regardless of gender, likely makes *all* the youth involved uncomfortable and puts the transgender youth at more risk. However, the transgender teen probably has friends within the larger group. It may be best and safest to place the transgender teen with friends they already trust and in whose company they feel most comfortable. Perhaps placing friends together, regardless of gender, may be the best solution to make everyone feel safe.

But how will you know around whom the LGBTQ youth are most comfortable? Before you make any decisions about housing, talk to the LGBTQ youth directly and privately. Ask questions about how they identify and how comfortable they are around other youth. Let them tell you around whom they feel the most and least comfortable. Let them propose possible housing solutions to you, solutions that may be much more innovative than you or I could come up with on our own. If possible, talk with the youth's parents and find out what aspect of the church trip concerns them most and what solutions they have come up with at home.

If you have a long-term relationship with the LGBTQ youth—meaning they aren't new to your church or your youth ministry—you may already know which youth are comfortable and which feel some tension in one another's company. Even then, it's still worth the conversation, just to double-check and be sure. If youth are new to the youth ministry, then such a conversation is essential to make sure that the LGBTQ youth and parents know that you are committed to their safety and well-being.

You also need to reinforce the rules and values of your church community. Talk about what sort of community you want to form. Talk about how each person in your youth ministry is created in the image of God. Talk about honoring one another as a child of God. Communicate clearly that harassment of any kind will not be tolerated. Talk about sexual ethics and healthy relationships for all your youth. Explicitly state a prohibition on sexual activity, regardless of the coupling. Even in the modest ways your gathering does allow interactions, you can reinforce the practice of consent and healthy relationships. And you can talk with youth and parents about how all of these concepts apply to the specific trip you are planning.

There is not going to be one perfect solution to housing and sleeping arrangements. There are too many variables and factors, including the very real variable of human emotions. But you can establish a framework that helps you plan and make decisions that are in the best interests of all the youth who participate in your ministry. You can state and reinforce your congregational values and let those values guide your planning process. You can communicate early and often with LGBTQ youth and their families about your values and listen to their hopes, concerns, and proposals. You can model acceptance and affirmation for the whole youth ministry. You can pay attention to youth interactions, noting who are the strongest allies and best role models for other youth.

While doing all this, you can pray for wisdom in all your ministry, asking God to guide you as you prepare and plan for a trip or camp that will be transformative for the youth and families involved.

CHAPTER

19

I'VE DIVIDED YOUTH INTO SMALL GROUPS BY GENDER—WHAT SHOULD I DO NOW?

At summer camp, we divided our morning Bible study session into two parts, unimaginatively called "large group" and "small group." The large group was typically facilitated by one or two people who would introduce the text and provide any relevant background on the Scripture passage. More often than not, the flow of communication in the large group was one way; youth could ask questions or respond to thoughts, but there was certainly a large-group, lecture-style dynamic.

The large-group Bible study ended with the leaders asking a few questions and then dividing the youth into smaller groups for more personal discussions. We gave these smaller groups a series of prompts to get the campers to interpret the text, talk about their lives and experiences, and react to one another. We counselors often just asked a couple opening questions and let the conversation flow where the Spirit led it, typically from the themes of the Scripture passages into the youths' own lives.

Splitting into small groups made it easier for campers to tell stories about their lives and experiences. Acknowledging that young people are often ignored in society, we wanted to make sure that our campers had the opportunity to tell us the truth about their lives. Our job was to prompt them and then sit back and listen.

Sometimes, we used the age gap between the campers and counselors to our advantage. It allowed us to ask questions to learn about what challenges our campers were facing, especially if they were different from what we had faced. We also asked them what tools and resources they had found to help them. This practice worked simply because we were genuinely interested in their lives. We asked questions in order to understand them and learn about them.

Sometimes the group wasn't chatty, and it was difficult to elicit their comments and responses. And sometimes the campers were so into the conversation that they were oblivious to the lunch bell.

How did we split up the youth? Each day was different, guided by different priorities. On the first day, our intention was to make sure that the youth who already knew each other before camp were in different groups and that campers had the opportunity to meet and get to hear from someone new. By the second day, we had realized that we had a handful of strong personalities and decided the best way to divide our small groups was to put the quiet kids together, allowing them the opportunity to speak, and to put the strong personalities together, forcing them to sort out their pecking order.

During our first summer, while we were being filmed for a documentary about our camp, the crew observed that after two days, the boys weren't connecting with one another. Instead, each one was latching on to one of the girl campers and was being much more open and friendly with them than they were with campers of their own gender. The film crew suggested dividing our campers into boys' and girls' groups (admittedly, a very gender-binary division). They thought that might provide opportunities to talk in greater depth with the youth about gender-specific issues, especially those issues that tend to emerge with puberty.

We were a little skeptical. The film crew had already suggested we do a few things simply to look dramatic for the camera. Earlier in the week, they had convinced us to hold a ceremony in which we raised a rainbow flag on the flagpole over the camp, just so they could capture it on film. They had even bought us the flag, so we didn't have an excuse. We had never thought that such a ceremony would be any part of our camp, but the film crew convinced us it would be visually dramatic, so we awkwardly clipped the flag in place and pulled the rope as campers looked upward. Meanwhile, the adult leaders were rolling our eyes the whole time.

The gendered small group division, however, worked brilliantly. It created an opportunity for youth to talk without embarrassment about personal issues that were more specific to each gender.

We stated the observation that the boys weren't getting as close to one another as the boys were to the girls. One boy responded by saying that he was nervous about becoming friends with other boys.

"What if that friendship turned into attraction?" he worried. "And what if that attraction wasn't reciprocated?"

In the campers' minds, it was far better to maintain a friendly distance than allow friendship to turn into a crush and then rejection.

We heard their concerns but also reminded them that this community was intended to help and support them. There was always the risk of developing feelings for another camper, and there would always be the risk of rejection. But by being open with one another, the boys could possibly find support and solidarity in an otherwise ambivalent and hostile world. Of course, in reality, we cannot force any relationships. But we did want to offer some encouragement to take the relationship risk.

After that first year, we kept the gender-identity groups as one variation of how we divided the youth into small groups. We realized that the third day was the best time in the flow of the camp week to break up into gendered groups.

If you have been dividing discussion groups by gender on occasion, I suggest you keep doing it. Contrary to what you might have heard, gender is important, which is why spending time talking and thinking about it is also so important. Many of us, especially cisgender people, never spend time thinking about our gender or the assumptions that come with it. It's only when we violate a culturally imposed gender norm that we end up thinking about what implications our gender has for how we are treated. What proactive small church or camp groups based on gender identity can do is encourage youth to think about the assumptions they have been taught about their gender and about how they can live an authentic life that reflects how God made them rather than who they have been told they are.

But then the question becomes, How do you implement the division?

For our first couple of years, we had so few youth and very little diversity of gender identity that we broke up into "boy" and "girl" groups. Once we had more campers and the range of gender identities expanded, we offered three options. One group was the male/boy/man/masculine group, another was the female/girl/woman/feminine group. The third group was for those who fell in between or outside the other groups. We gave this group a squishy label, describing it as the "transgender/gender-nonconforming/genderqueer group."

During our summer camp, this was the only day we allowed the youth to choose which group to join. We set it up in a very careful way. We let them know that we wanted to split up into gender-identity groups. We also talked about our limitations of physical space and our logistics. We were not a big group, and we had a limited number of adult leaders. We told them that there were three options from which they could choose (as explained earlier) and that we would make those options available by location.

You might think that the third group was for all the transgender youth, but transgender youth actually have more choices when gendered groups are set up this way. Some of our transgender youth didn't want to dwell on their transgender status. They wanted to talk about what it means to be a boy or a girl, because that is how they see themselves and who they are. Some youth who were more fluid, genderqueer, nonbinary, or even just early on in exploring their gender identity could choose the third group. But of course, no one can be in more than one room at the same time. And to build trust within each group, we didn't let youth move between groups after we got going.

Gendered group discussions could go in several different directions. Sometimes, as adult leaders, we asked questions like, "What is the biggest pressure associated with your gender?" This would often prompt a discussion of expectations and stereotypes that our campers faced and how they dealt with it. Sometimes, the discussion turned toward bodies and health. Youth talked about dealing with body issues for being too skinny, too fat, underdeveloped, overdeveloped, and so on. We also asked what they liked about their gender, prompting a conversation about what they enjoyed, an examination of privilege, and an affirmation of who they are, whether as boys, girls, nonbinary, genderqueer, or whatever.

Some of the prompts we used to launch gender-identity group questions included the following:

- What is the best part about your gender?
- What's the most challenging part about your gender?
- How did you figure out your gender (a question you can ask all youth, not just the transgender ones)?
- What is something people assume about you because of your gender that isn't true?
- How do you combat stereotypes about your gender?

This is also a good time for youth to learn from each other and from adult leaders about puberty, health issues to watch out for, and legal, social, or administrative barriers or opportunities they may be facing. Sometimes, youth have questions about "how things work" in relation to a variety of topics: menstrual products, hormone blockers, supportive resources, and so on. Sometimes older youth who have been through a similar experience can share their wisdom, and sometimes adult leaders can provide information or pledge to help research answers to a question.

We sometimes found that the gender-identity group discussion had such resonance that it ended too soon. In such cases, one of our counselors would offer to continue the conversation during a later free time. Logan, who had a background in leading workshops on gender identity and queer theory, fielded youth questions and listened to them talk about their lives and experiences.

At one point, Logan approached us to say that in one group, they had two distinct sets of campers who wanted to continue talking about gender identity. One set was made up of youth who were under the transgender umbrella in some way. They had questions related to their own lives, what they should do, what resources are available, and what to expect. The members of the other group were not transgender, but they had questions about transgender people or the transgender experience. Because Logan had offered themself as someone who would patiently listen and respond to any question, youth wanted to take advantage of that. But it was dividing Logan's attention: while Logan focused on one group, the other felt alienated.

This is important learning for you as you lead discussions about gender identity in small groups. First, *all* youth should learn about gender identity, not just the transgender youth. Second, youth should have an opportunity to explore and discuss the implications of their own gender identity but will also be eager to learn about the realities of gender identities other than their own.

Your paramount consideration should be the safety needed to allow youth to trust a small group with questions about the implications of their own gender. This may not be the time to ask questions about someone else's gender identity. Instead, realize that youth are asking very personal questions, still sorting out how God made them and what that means for living in a world that (generally) does not fully embrace them as a created and beloved child of God. You will need to be as frank as you can about the barriers they may face and what they need to do to overcome those barriers.

When learning about other people's gender identity, it helps to recognize that we don't have all the language to ask questions correctly and properly. So Logan would start discussions by saying, "We don't have the perfect language to ask what we need to know, and if you have a question, I want you to be able to ask it without being worried you'll offend me. I will assume that you have good intentions in however you word something. However, because I care, I will tell you a better way to phrase the question." Have folks on hand who can respond to most questions and who have experience with understanding the range of gender identity. But know that there is always a limit to personal knowledge, and remind folks that we are all learning about this together (even when we are learning about ourselves).

In the end, remind youth once again that we are all created in God's image, are known intimately by God, and are loved by God, even as we grow and discover more about ourselves. By creating a safe space where youth and adults can talk honestly, figure things out together, and learn from one another, we are creating educated and informed allies who can share the love of God for creation with others who need to hear it.

CHAPTER

20

HOW CAN WE QUEER THE YOUTH MINISTRY EXPERIENCE?

Seeing this chapter's title, I imagine you saying, "Whoa, whoa, whoa! When I was a kid, 'queer' was an insult. Why would I want to call my youth ministry 'queer'?" But perhaps by now you trust me enough to go along with my suggestions just a little longer. Yes, *queer* has been used as an insult. But it has always had a variety of meanings, including as a term of empowerment.

Have you heard your kids use *queer* as an insult? Have you heard your kids use *queer* as an identity?[1]

Historically, the word has meant "eccentric" or "odd." "There's nowt so queer as folk" is a northern phrase that means that nothing is as strange as people.[2] The word *queer* started being applied to what we might now call LGBTQ people in the early twentieth century. Radclyffe Hall was a Christian writer who preferred the word *invert* to describe herself.[3] In her 1928 book, *The Well of Loneliness*, she used religious language to support the inclusion of LGBTQ people. For example, its protagonist, similarly a gender-nonconforming "invert" like Hall, has a dream "that in some queer way she was Jesus."[4]

Queer became a pejorative term over the course of the twentieth century, a term used to insult people who didn't fit into society's dominant gender or orientation expectations. We can see the relationship between the original meaning—"weird" or "strange"—and this use of the word as an insult.

To use the word *queer* and mean it as an insult for a particular group of people is to follow a set of assumptions as a form of logic—namely, that

- heterosexuality is normal,
- masculinity is normal (but only for men),
- femininity is normal (but only for women), and
- everything else is weird (queer).

The biggest underlying assumption of this logic is that that "normal" is good and that "weird" is bad. Once you assume this, the rest follows.

But what if you start to question those assumptions? What if heterosexuality wasn't normal for everyone? What if masculinity wasn't normal for all men and femininity wasn't normal for all women? What is "normal" anyway?

Most importantly, what if your assumptions turn out to be radically different from your values?

Once you start to question assumptions, you can take a queer perspective to anything. *To queer* and *queering* mean questioning what is "normal" for the assumptions we take for granted, especially around gender and sexuality (and other things too). Biblical scholars have queered (or queried or questioned) Scripture. Political activists have queered community organizing and politics. Academics have queered history, philosophy, art, and the rest of the humanities.

So why not also queer or question your youth ministry? That's what this book does. The focus on values rather than logistics is a way of peeling back and questioning the assumptions of how we run things. The most basic assumption that you've already been asking is, "What if we don't assume everyone is straight and cisgender?"

How do we go about queering our youth ministry? One way is to queer our existing practices. Take a game I played as a youth, Chuck Charlie, which, I realized, is actually a really queer game. Here's how I explained it:

While holding up a pillow, I say, "This is Charlie. At the beginning of the game, Charlie doesn't have many friends, only two. But those two want the rest of us to become 'friends of Charlie.' How are they going to do that? Well, once those two hit us with the pillow (below the neck, for safety's sake), we will be converted and become a fellow 'friend of Charlie.' Once you are a friend of Charlie, your goal changes from avoiding being hit by Charlie (again, below the neck!) to trying to recruit others into being a friend of Charlie. The twist is that when you are holding Charlie in your arms, your feet cannot move. So when you aren't holding Charlie, you can run close to someone else and yell, 'Chuck Charlie!' and your fellow friend of Charlie will throw Charlie over to you, so you can tag someone else with Charlie and make them a fellow friend. By the end of the game, we will *all* be friends of Charlie!"

This is precisely how I explained the game of Chuck Charlie while working at a church camp in college. Yet standing in front of a group of LGBTQ youth made me realize how the understanding of the game was completely different. Chuck Charlie is a game about recruiting people to become "friends of Charlie."

What's queer about that? The predator is a painful stereotype with which many LGBTQ people grew up. Anti-LGBTQ activists and even a portion of well-meaning people portray LGBTQ persons as needing to "recruit" others into their "lifestyle," especially young people. This game of Chuck Charlie turns that stereotype on its head and strips it of its power. Remember, we are talking about a pillow. The pillow can't convert people any more than LGBTQ people can. And yet we have given the pillow a name and called those on the pillow's team "friends of Charlie." The game exposes the absurdity of the stereotype and mocks it, even while eliciting strategy, exercise, and teamwork. It's a reclaiming of a nasty stigma, much like reclaiming the word *queer* itself.

Sometimes, to queer a game, you just need to add a queer twist. Take kickball. What could possibly be queer about kickball? Brad had friends who would often put a show tunes twist on standard sports. Any time someone would make a goal, shoot a basket, or do anything that earned points, they would be required to sing a show tune before the points were granted. Brad applied this principle to the concept of traditional kickball and thus invented show tunes kickball.

He stood before our youth and, with great confidence that didn't betray the fact that he was making up the game on the spot, explained the rules of show tunes kickball. In nearly every way, the game would have the same rules as regular kickball. A camper would kick a rolling ball and run around the three bases to score a point. However, in our version, the player needed to sing a song from musical theater between third base and home. If you weren't singing, the point wouldn't count.

"And," Brad declared with the voice of authority, "if you repeat a show tune that has already been sung in the game, you are *out!*"

We gasped.

Show tunes kickball was a way to take a traditional game and make it just a little more queer. But it did more than that. It changed the balance of power in the playing field. For youth who have lived through the experience of being picked last for kickball in high school because their interests were in the arts rather than athletics, the game gave them an ego boost. That not every youth could name a show tune made those with a knowledge of musical theater that much more valuable to the team.

Of course, traditional athletic ability is still valued in this game. One still needs to be able to kick and to run to third base, where a singing voice and catalog of musical theater are needed. Some youth kick the ball and run quickly around the bases, stopping suddenly at third base because they don't know what to sing for the last leg of their journey.

Eventually, we allowed teams to install a "third-base coach" who would quickly teach a player the chorus to a song before the next ball was kicked. Sometimes, a youth would stay on third for an extra kick, just to make sure they understood and remembered the song. But eventually, the bases would get backed up, and they were forced to make the run, screaming out the lyrics of a recently learned show tune as they crossed home plate.

Over time, we had to examine and clarify the rules regarding what songs would qualify as a legitimate show tune. For our purposes, we determined that jukebox musicals were allowed. Disney songs were allowed only if the show and its songs had been staged on Broadway. However, songs featured in films or television shows didn't count unless they were from Broadway musicals. This last rule answered what we called the "*Glee* dilemma," *Glee* being a show popular among teenagers that featured songs from a variety of genres, most of which didn't come from Broadway musicals.

If you are lucky and your youth ministry is sufficiently LGBTQ inclusive, eventually you will have someone who performs in drag. Drag is a form of performance art in which the performer takes on a character, often of a different gender. It is not the same thing as transgender identity but rather a costume for the purpose of performance. When you understand that distinction, you can incorporate a drag performance into a talent show, youth outing, or, if you are bold enough, worship.

Some of the youth who attended our summer camp did drag performances. One boy, Dain, came to camp with an entire cosmetic case of drag makeup as well as a couple of different outfits. He spent the afternoon giving tutorials on makeup and hair to campers who wanted to listen and learn. On the day of our talent show, he was helping others with makeup. Some were going to try drag for the first time, but many of the campers wanted makeup just to try something new. He made the experience so fun that others wanted to join in. Every participant, youth and adult, even those who had no personal interest in drag, wanted to sample his makeup expertise, since it was a new experience. That year, all the adult leaders were modeling the perfect "smoky-eye" eyeliner effect while still wearing shorts and sweatshirts.

If it's done well, playing with drag or gender expression can be a fun experience for all your youth, not just the LGBTQ youth. It also allows youth to queer their own style or expression.

Another way we've done such queering is through the casual activity of painting fingernails. We buy inexpensive nail polish, cotton swabs, polish remover, and so on and sit at picnic tables to paint our own or another person's nails while we chat with one another. Some youth change their polish every day; others keep it on until the end of camp or beyond. Guys who were told they shouldn't enjoy fingernail polish got to experience it, perhaps for the first time. Some painted a single nail, others a full rainbow. Remember, fingernail polish isn't gender specific. Painting our nails is another way to prompt a conversation about gender roles and gender expression.

Perhaps the biggest way that you can queer a youth ministry program is to empower members of your community to share the queer wisdom they have learned in their lives. During one of Greg's first years leading The Naming Project, I asked him to lead the campfire. Greg didn't come from a church camp background. Without a lot of preconceived notions about how campfires were "supposed" to work, Greg developed a message unlike any I had seen before. Greg was a huge fan of Dolly Parton. He liked her music, her philanthropy, and her message that mixed Christian devotion with self-acceptance. He wanted to share with the campers some of the messages that Dolly had imparted.

Greg set up a speaker outside the campfire ring. He began by reading some of Dolly's most poignant quotations without identifying their source. After a couple of quotations about self-acceptance, he asked the campers who might have said such affirmations. The campers named some of the most popular figures, including Lady Gaga, Katy Perry, and Beyoncé. None of the campers was familiar with Dolly or her wisdom. Greg then talked about what an inspiration Dolly had been for him personally. He talked about her upbringing in a poor community, how she combines an over-the-top persona with humble roots, and how she uses her sense of humor and her history to help others.

Greg then played some songs by Dolly Parton, including "Jesus and Gravity," in which Dolly sings about being lifted up by Christ while staying humble here on earth. He then played "Travelin' Through," the song written for the film *Transamerica*, which tells the story of a transgender woman reconnecting with her son from deep in her past in a cross-country journey that brings them together. The song is a spiritual, talking about being a pilgrim on this earth; living through both joys and challenges; being in various relationships with family, friends, and significant others; and even being transformed by our relationships and experiences, all while being loved by the God who created us, knows us, and loves us.

Greg's "Gospel According to Dolly" became a tradition at our camp, and it soon merged with another tradition. Bay Lake Camp staff told us that we could take the pontoon boat out onto the lake in the evening to watch the sunset and view the stars. We took them up on their offer and developed a "pontoon campfire." Campers and staff piled into a pontoon, and we drove out into the middle of the water before cutting the engine. For the fire, we lit tealights and votive candles in jars. Some years, we handed out glow sticks to all the campers.

It was in this boat at the setting of the sun and the emergence of the stars that Greg would tell the campers about the "Gospel According to Dolly." He would read a handful of her quotes, finding new ones each year that connected with our Scripture theme. He talked about how Dolly has lived out her values and her faith, even while being known for being flamboyant and busty. He always played "Jesus and Gravity" and "Travelin' Through" as staples but added additional songs that matched the Bible study theme of the week.

The tradition of a Dolly Parton pontoon campfire wasn't like anything I'd experienced at a camp before. It's a completely different experience than sitting around a blazing fire on land. We'd sing songs, our voices carrying across the water. Then Greg would play Dolly, and her voice would carry across the water, mixing with ours.

It queered the campfire experience.

While we float each year, I imagine Jesus on his own fishing boat, with his voice carrying across the water as he preached to the crowds. He wasn't talking about Dolly Parton, but he was telling stories of farmers and seeds, planting and cultivating, comparing our faith lives and their challenges to agriculture and the many ways in which crops can thrive or fail. These stories were told from a boat so that the message could be heard by many people, just like our songs and stories would spread over the water to be heard by those sharing the lake with us.

Queering can happen to games, traditions, routines, meals, and liturgies. There is nothing that we do regularly that should be shielded from examining what we do and whether it upholds our values. It's worth asking these questions just to decide what value you get from activities or actions. You may decide that there is still great value for the community in what you do. Great! Then keep it. But if you find ways to tweak and adjust the program, you may be enacting an even more effective ministry.

CHAPTER

21

WHAT ABOUT QUEERING YOUTH MINISTRY SONGS?

Sung only by the manliest bro-type counselors—buff college jocks who relished primal screaming—the popular camp song "Vista" intimidated me as a camper, a closeted, skinny, gay boy. No wonder that when I became a camp counselor, I avoided leading "Vista." It was a song for someone more masculine than I was. When we started The Naming Project, I didn't even consider the song as a part of my repertoire.

That changed one year. I was working with a cadre of new counselors, good people who were unfamiliar with the specific routine of our camp. That year, I did more heavy lifting of the camp program, and for some reason, "Vista" popped into my head and how the counselors who had led the song when I was a youth had intimidated me. I decided to reclaim the song. I decided to strip it of its power over my self-perception as not sufficiently masculine for the song.

None of the youth or adult leaders had heard the song before, so I told them to slap their laps and clap in a slow rhythm and echo back at me whatever I yelled at them. And then, using that same scream that I had heard as a camper, I let out a primal, "*Veeeee!*" The echo came back, a strong "*Veeeee!*"

"Vee vay!" I called.

"Vee vay!" they answered.

"Vee vay vo!"

"Vee vay vo!"

Then, in what I imagined to be a loud, husky, manly whisper, "Vista!"

Instead of a matching husky whisper, one of the adult leaders, Pastor Megan, squealed, "Vista!" and raised her arms over her head, like the completion of a cheerleading pose. It was more than I could handle, and I broke out laughing, along with the rest of the camp.

And just like that, the hold "Vista" had had over me was broken. We had queered "Vista." It was no longer a song signifying masculinity. It was no longer a song that was off limits to me. It was a song that evoked laughter, joy, and silliness.

Perhaps the songwriter had never intended the song to be intimidating, but it had become so somewhere between the camp where I grew up and my own internalized homophobia.

We continue to sing "Vista," primal screams and all.

The last line of the stanza now evokes the most laughs, because no one, including me, is completely sure what the lyrics are supposed to be. By the last line, we're supposed to have worked ourselves into a frenzy, and I yell out something like, "Ish biddley, oaten goaten, bobost code eaten noten!" Most youth and adult leaders have no idea what I'm saying and respond with a mishmash of words approximating the sounds I've made.

Those words are a rough approximation of what I learned as a child. Were they nonsense words? Were they taken from another language and bastardized beyond recognition? Who knows! The purpose of the song is to enjoy ourselves, laugh, and expend energy at the beginning of a campfire gathering.

But the masculinity of songs continues to pose challenges. Church music across history, from Gregorian chants to Christian death metal, tends to use masculine language. Traditional youth ministry and camp songs are no different. The language for God and for people has been male centric for so long that it's easy to be unaware of it. As a white male being taught these songs, I didn't think about how women and people of color would hear lyrics that leave them out of the vision of God about which we sing. But as an adult gay man trying to convey to campers the expansiveness of God's identity, I became more aware of how narrow our church song language is. This is the God whom Moses encountered at his own version of a campfire, a burning bush. God speaks to Moses from the fire, recounting the suffering of God's people. Moses asks of God, "If I come to the Israelites and say to them, 'The God of your ancestors has sent me to you,' and they ask me, 'What is his name?' what shall I say to them?" God's response to Moses is, "I am who I am."[1] The Hebrew words spoken here don't translate easily into English. Other correct translations include "I am what I am" or "I will be what I will be."[2]

At no point in this story does God refer to God's own self as exclusively male. People applied male language *to* God as time went on, referring to God as "King" and "Father," and that same exclusive language has largely dominated the language of our singing ever since.

I liked many of the songs with which I grew up. They had good energy, they were easy to teach, and probably most important to me, I knew how to play and sing them. I still wanted to use them at The Naming Project. But I didn't want to refer to God only as "Father" or "King." Even "Lord" made me uncomfortable. And most of all, I didn't want to use "he" pronouns exclusively to talk about God.

God, creator of heaven and earth, cannot be constrained by labels and language. Neither should our campers be constrained by exclusionary and discriminatory language. Creating a safe and welcoming place also has to do with what songs we sing and the language they use for God and for people.

There are a few ways that you can address noninclusive youth church music:

- Learn new songs.

    Some songs are simply too male, cisgender, and heterosexual dominant to be salvaged for a truly LGBTQ-inclusive youth ministry. There are too many inclusive songs out there to stay stuck in the same repertoire. When you find a song loaded with "Father" or "King" language, it may be time to hold that song up to the values you hold as a community and ask your-self how a young LGBTQ person might interpret the song. Will they feel excluded if the song doesn't represent masculinity the way they understand themselves? Beyond LGBTQ youth, will a youth whose father is absent or abusive find such joy in a song that names God as the ultimate father?

If we look just beyond our own traditions and denominations, we can find a vast range of songs that colorfully and imaginatively praise God. These songs imagine God's nurturing side or invoke the Holy Spirit. I'm thinking of songs like "Gathered Here in the Mystery of the Hour," "Come, Let Us Worship God," "Peace before Us," "Up above My Head," and "It's a Blessing You Were Born" that you can find on the internet.

At The Naming Project, we had adult leaders from a variety of Chris-tian and spiritual backgrounds who had learned more inclusive songs than I knew. Logan had been a part of intentional Christian communities and worship spaces. He taught us songs and chants that celebrated the com-munity gathered in Christ, songs about God's call for justice in the world, and songs calling for the Spirit to fall upon our community. Some of these songs were new, some were new to me, and some were centuries old. Another counselor, Conie, was a part of Music That Makes Community, a faith-based nonprofit that empowers and liberates spiritual life through singing.[3] The music she taught our camp inspired movement, was deeply meditative, and was also very fun to sing.

- Change the language within the song.

    You might also modify the language within existing popular songs. Let the youth know ahead of time that your practice will be to switch up the pronouns for God, and remind them that it limits our sense of God and God's creation to use such limited vocabulary. Use "he," "she," or "they," and sometimes just alternate between them, even within the same song. Youth can use whichever they like.

    Still, to keep the rhythm and musicality, be mindful of syllables and sense. Replacing "Father" with "Creator" doesn't work well, but "Mother,"

"Parent," and "Maker" work. It takes some intentionality and some creativity, but it can be done.

This is the option I tend to use the most. I let campers know that I will be switching and mixing up pronouns as I teach and sing a song, and then I'm intentional about changing up the pronouns in the midst of a song. There is a bit of holy chaos that happens when we get to a pronoun and some of us say "he," while others say "she," and still others "they." But gender is a bit of holy chaos, so we embrace it.

• Write your own songs.

Perhaps the most creative and queerest thing you can do with your praise is write your own songs to reflect your relationship with God—songs not borrowed from someone else's perspective or experience but that articulate how you experience God.

With a friend, I'd written a camp song titled "FripFrop" while working at a church camp in my college years. On a dare, we created the song in the middle of leading campers through morning worship. It was a dumb song without much theological depth, but others later refined and developed it, and it continues to be sung at that same camp.

I regularly challenge youth to write their own youth ministry songs. No one has done so yet, but there are plenty of youth with amazing musical talent, and it'd be great to sing their compositions.

Queering youth songs isn't about throwing out your songbook and starting from scratch. It means looking at your values and checking that what you sing upholds those values. Not every song has to have profound theological depth. Like "FripFrop," many of our songs don't. But you can examine the songs you sing in community. You can expand your repertoire with songs that come from outside your faith tradition. You can add a queer twist to existing, popular songs. You can even write new songs that reflect your unique community and its unique relationship to God. Praising God with words that reflect God's, yours, and your community's fullness is surely worth that extra bit of work.

CHAPTER

22

DOES THIS MEAN LGBTQ YOUTH MIGHT CHANGE MY BIBLE STUDY?

You may have heard it said that LGBTQ Christians ignore the Bible to suit their own interests. I hope that by this point in the book, you realize how seriously LGBTQ Christians—and by extension, your LGBTQ youth—take Scripture.

The problem is that the discussion of LGBTQ people and Scripture has been limited to a handful of verses that some people interpret as opposing LGBTQ identity. I, for one, am tired of talking about what Leviticus does or does not mean, what Paul really means at the end of the first chapter of Romans, or what really happened to Sodom and Gomorrah. It's a tired, old discussion that hasn't done anything for anyone's faith. Let's expand our scriptural horizons!

"But," you say, "there aren't any LGBTQ people in the Bible. So to whom can LGBTQ youth relate?"

It's a commonly held misperception that LGBTQ people don't appear in the Bible. It's probably more accurate to say that our culture and society condition us not to see the LGBTQ experience in Scripture. When LGBTQ people lived in the closet far away from open discussion in churches and seminaries, interpretation of biblical texts was strictly enforced through a heteronorma-tive lens. The assumption was that every single character was heterosexual and cisgender.

Today, LGBTQ people are much more visible at school, at work, at church, and in the world. Youth in your church may already identify as a part of the LGBTQ community. Both the LGBTQ and youth experiences provide different sets of lenses through which to read the stories, poems, letters, and songs written in Scripture. Their real, everyday experience in the world is going to influence what details they pick up on in Scripture. It's going to shape how and to which characters and stories they relate. In short, it's going to change how they interpret the Bible. This is a good thing! Chris-tians believe that the Bible is more than just an old set of writings, made for a different time and place but something relevant to our lives today. Allow LGBTQ youth to perceive Scripture as relevant to their lives.

This new and queer perspective on Scripture challenges how the church has interpreted these stories and passages in the past and how we teach Scrip-ture today. If that sentence sounds frightening, it shouldn't be. As Christians, we should be used to the Bible and specifically Jesus challenging the wisdom of the world. The message of the cross and the resurrection of Christ upended the way we understand the world. In his first letter to the Corinthians, Paul made this point quite emphatically:

> For the message about the cross is foolishness to those who are per-ishing, but to us who are being saved it is the power of God. For it is written,
>
> > "I will destroy the wisdom of the wise,
> > and the discernment of the discerning I will thwart."
>
> Where is the one who is wise? Where is the scribe? Where is the debater of this age? Has not God made foolish the wisdom of the world? For since, in the wisdom of God, the world did not know God through wisdom, God decided, through the foolishness of our

proclamation, to save those who believe. For Jews demand signs and Greeks desire wisdom, but we proclaim Christ crucified, a stumbling block to Jews and foolishness to Gentiles, but to those who are the called, both Jews and Greeks, Christ the power of God and the wisdom of God. For God's foolishness is wiser than human wisdom, and God's weakness is stronger than human strength.[1]

Jesus's death and resurrection overturned—or queered—what was considered conventional wisdom about a savior. Logically, God coming to earth only to die makes no sense. It runs counter to the notions of power that humankind associates with God. And yet it is the core of our Christian belief. If we can accept that the wisdom of God seems like foolishness to us, then we can be open to the wild ways in which LGBTQ youth can see themselves and their lives reflected in the Bible.

First, a caveat: imposing our modern understanding of what is meant by gay, lesbian, bisexual, or transgender on a biblical character doesn't work. Those are all terms that no one in biblical times would have used to describe themselves. But that doesn't mean the experiences and emotions biblical characters had can't inform how a young LGBTQ person will understand the world around them.

I once led a Bible study on Esther for The Naming Project. Esther's story is epic, filled with heroes and villains, intrigue, and attempted genocide. It reminds me of a big epic musical, like *Les Misérables*, and that's how I presented it to the camp youth. I did a retelling of Esther, enlisting youth to act—or sing—out the parts of Esther, Mordecai, Haman, and King Ahasuerus. The plot of Esther is relatively straightforward. Esther is a young Jewish girl living under the rule of a foreign king. The king has deposed his queen, deeming her insubordinate for refusing to humiliate herself in front of him and his court. He is looking for someone to replace her. Enter Esther. King Ahasuerus is quite taken with her and makes her his new queen.[2]

But Queen Esther has a secret. She is Jewish and living under occupation in the Persian Empire. This makes her a religious and ethnic minority, one now placed in a high-profile position. Xenophobia runs as deep in the Bible as it does today.

How many LGBTQ people have been held in high esteem yet have felt pressure to keep their sexual orientation and gender identity secret? For the youth who may be discovering their sexual orientation or gender identity, coming out—or worse, being outed involuntarily—might make everything they've built come crashing down. They too have been the delight of their family, church, school, or community. They too have held positions of influence: captain of the football team, class president, Sunday school teacher, and so on. Adults and peers alike praise them for their leadership, but the youth continues to think, deep down, "If they only knew . . ." Some youth legitimately fear being kicked out of their home or church, losing the respect of their peers, being bullied or harassed, and so on. These youth may easily understand what sort of pressure Esther is facing.

Her uncle, Mordecai, advises Esther not to "come out" about her identity as a Jew. Mordecai has been through a lot. He's seen the ways in which the king can be cruel to outsiders. In the same way, LGBTQ adults know how cruel the world can be and often worry for the youth. We carry our own scars and memories, and while we hope that life will be better for the next generation, we are wary.

When Mordecai overhears a plot to kill all the Jews, the stakes are raised. Now Esther is facing the dilemma of whether she should come out. If she stays in the closet, she will remain safe, but her people will die. If she comes out, she risks facing xenophobia, bigotry, and violence head-on. She could lose her position of power and be killed along with her people. But there is the smallest possibility that she might save her fellow Jews.

Esther's task is to figure out how to come out in such a way that turns the king's heart away from the slander and stereotypes he's heard about her people. Her goal must be to save all the Jews, including herself.

I've been using the language of "coming out" when talking about Esther's dilemma. Am I calling Esther a lesbian? Bisexual? Queer? The honest answer is, "I don't know." But I do know that LGBTQ people understand deeply the difficulty of when and how to come out. Most LGBTQ youth have asked themselves very similar questions. Think back to John, who planned a gay-la to strengthen his resolve before coming out. Think of what your youth might consider the consequences of coming out. The characters don't have to be explicitly LGBTQ for their stories and feelings to be relatable for LGBTQ youth.

This LGBTQ youth identification with biblical characters goes beyond coming out. Remember Naomi, Ruth's mother-in-law? Both women had lost their husbands and are facing the dire prospect of living as two widows in a culture that doesn't value widows. They are also living in a foreign land, far from any kin who might take them in. Naomi urges Ruth to return to her own people so she can be cared for, but Ruth refuses. She eventually utters a promise we have repeated during Christian wedding ceremonies:

> Do not press me to leave you
>> or to turn back from following you!
> Where you go, I will go;
>> where you lodge, I will lodge;
> your people shall be my people,
>> and your God my God.[3]

Many LGBTQ youth are astonished to learn that this Bible verse, which is frequently quoted in marriage ceremonies, is a statement of commitment uttered by one woman to another. Quite honestly, most adults are astonished as well. Having heard that verse in a heterosexual wedding repeatedly has made us forget from where the story comes. Until marriage equality was the law of the land in the United States, the verse was being used out of the context of the story. The commitment is not one between a husband and wife but between a mother-in-law and daughter-in-law.

The fact that Naomi's pledge isn't a wedding vow doesn't strip it of its power. It is a promise to stick together, to support one another. Naomi knows they will be stronger together than they would be apart. Our LGBTQ youth recognize this commitment and perhaps see a future for themselves in which they are surrounded by loving, caring people who pledge to support one another. Maybe it will be a single special someone to whom they can commit their life . . . or perhaps it will be the idea of a "chosen family," the network of nonbiological relationships that sustain us. Those relationships don't need to be romantic or sexual to be mutual and fulfilling. It makes the pledge no less powerful than when Ruth said it to Naomi.

Stories like this can give LGBTQ youth a glimpse of what their lives and their futures could be like. It gives them hope. They see how Ruth and Naomi's commitment and mutual support pay off in the end.

There are other Bible stories that challenge the rigid gender norms our youth are taught. Deborah was a judge. Lydia was a business owner and the head of a household. Both held positions reserved for men, both in Scripture and through much of history.

Joseph's story might be the most telling. (This is Joseph of Genesis, not Joseph the earthly father of Jesus. You may know him better as *Joseph and the Amazing Technicolor Dreamcoat*.) If you have siblings, you will recall the tensions you experienced, complete with fights over who is the parent's favorite. Joseph is the youngest of twelve brothers, and Genesis says that he is his father's favorite. The other brothers' resentment is already stirring when Genesis adds the detail that "Joseph brought a bad report of them to their father."[4] So Joseph is a tattletale. Not helpful with family dynamics!

Their father gives Joseph a garment, described in the New Revised Standard Version as "a long robe with sleeves."[5] This garment is the Technicolor dreamcoat of musical theater or the "coat of many colors" of Dolly Parton. Seeing where else in the Bible such a garment appears can be illuminating. Tamar, the daughter of King David, wears "a long robe with sleeves." But 2 Samuel adds this extra description: "For this is how the virgin daughters of the king were clothed in earlier times."[6] The word used for both those garments is the same in Hebrew. However, the description of Tamar's robe explicitly notes that she's wearing a garment designed for daughters of the king.

So is Joseph wearing a princess dress? I wasn't there, so it's not my place to say. However, for any young person who dressed up in clothes that didn't line up with their sex assigned at birth, for anyone who experimented with drag, for anyone who felt like the clothes chosen by their parents didn't fit who they were, Joseph is a biblical character with whom they can identify. Maybe, just maybe, Joseph shared their interest in dressing up . . . like a princess.

Then there's the reaction of Joseph's brothers. Is it driven not only by jealousy but also by shame that their brother is dressing in a gender-nonconforming way? That their genderqueer little brother was the father's favorite even though he was breaking all the norms and rules of the culture? Adding embarrassment and shame to an existing jealousy is like throwing gasoline on a fire.

Much later in Genesis, after Joseph has gone on a series of misadventures, he finds himself governing the Egyptian pharaoh's stockpile of food in a famine, selling it to the people who didn't or couldn't prepare. Those people include Joseph's own brothers. Joseph has grown up and changed considerably since his brothers last saw him, and they do not recognize him. He is dressed as an Egyptian governor. He is no longer the gender-nonconforming youngest born they knew but a powerful ruler with the ability to grant or deny life-giving resources to those who ask.

It is not only Joseph's appearance that has changed. His years in slavery, his time in prison, the hardship he's endured—all these have hardened him to the ways of the world. He has experienced both its cruelty and its beauty. He doesn't sound like the little dreamer his brothers knew. He sounds like someone who has experienced the joy and pain of the world.

The experience of not being recognized by those who knew us as children is one to which LGBTQ people can relate. This is especially true for transgender people, who may look significantly different than they did as children or youth. We have all gone from being dressed by others to expressing our gender on our own terms. We have been through trials and tribulations that make us a little more cynical and cautious. If you read this passage with older LGBTQ youth, you may hear them express solidarity with Joseph's experience.

These are only a couple of stories that can help you see how you can open up Scripture in a new way to all of us. There are many others: David and Jonathan, Moses, Paul, Jesus and "the beloved disciple," and so on.

It's worth exploring the character of Jesus a little further, since as Christians, Jesus is the central figure of our faith and the lens through which we read all of Scripture. Jesus is also a relatable figure for LGBTQ youth because so much of his life and his story defies expectations. He was conceived to a woman who was betrothed but not yet married, a cause for scandal in biblical times and still today. Jesus grew up with two dads: an earthly father who raised him and taught him carpentry and God his heavenly father. As far as we know, Jesus wasn't married, but he surrounded himself with chosen family, even referring to his disciples as "my mother and my brothers."[7] These are all experiences to which LGBTQ youth can relate.

Jesus doesn't stay within the categories and boundaries that we have established to order our world. Instead, Jesus embodies the "both/and" for categories like clean and unclean, human and divine, and even dead and alive.

Jesus points us to God. If Jesus defies boundaries and categories, what does that tell us about God?

The most common way the church describes God is as the Trinity, a concept that is nothing if not queer. Instead of a straightforward description of God, we get a tangle of relationships that cannot be separated and yet are distinct. No wonder the Athanasian Creed spends paragraphs trying to explain the unity of God while still describing the individual persons that make up the Trinity. All three persons are God, but they are distinct from one another. If you focus on any one part, you lose the understanding of the Trinity as a whole. It's messy, and it looks a lot like the internal feelings and external relationships LGBTQ youth have with friends, family, teachers, pastors, and community members.

When we open our eyes to how the experiences of LGBTQ youth can shape our own study of Scripture, we are transformed by their presence and their witness. Indeed, LGBTQ youth are a part of God's expansive, diverse, and expectation-defying creation because they teach the church something fundamental about the nature of our radical God.

I hope that these few biblical examples have reminded you of God's life-affirming calling. I hope you have found them liberating—for yourself and for your youth—and that the examples have expanded your idea of what God is like. I challenge you to ask your youth which biblical characters most resemble them. They may teach you to look at the Bible in a whole new way.

CHAPTER

23

WHAT ABOUT WORKING WITH OTHER MINISTRY ORGANIZATIONS THAT DON'T SHARE MY VALUES ABOUT LGBTQ PEOPLE?

C hurches partner with many organizations to enhance the congregational youth ministry: Organizations that provide all the infrastructure for a mission trip. Organizations that send teams of musicians to your congregation to sing contemporary Christian music and liven up weeknight church programming. Organizations that create service opportunities for you to pack food and deliver to a local food bank.

Many of these organizations are part of denominations and faith traditions that are not affirming of LGBTQ people. Many youth ministry organizations come from an evangelical background, and the bulk of their business comes from evangelical or nondenominational churches. Of course, not all evangelical churches are anti-LGBTQ, but the ones that are tend to be quite vocal about their beliefs and policies. These organizations likely align with an anti-LGBTQ worldview, or they know that they cannot publicly contradict such a worldview without harming their bottom line.

Making your youth ministry or your whole church safe and affirming for LGBTQ youth will mean ensuring that the ministries and service providers with whom you work are also affirming. This will not be easy. Parachurch youth ministry programs have slick, effective marketing. They are much more media savvy than mainline protestant denominations and our churches. They have created a bubble that will reinforce their worldview in television networks, magazines, contemporary Christian music, and well-produced events and retreats that will impress and attract you and your youth with every genre of music, multimedia, high production values, and entertaining and engaging big-name speakers.

Your work as an affirming youth leader is to make absolutely certain that whatever ministry or organization you are partnering with is as safe for LGBTQ youth as you strive to make your own youth ministry. This will mean asking hard questions.

An example: Let's say your church is partnering with a parachurch ministry that organizes mission trips to do disaster recovery work. The parachurch ministry handles your housing and meals, trains your youth group in the tasks they will be assigned, gets them out to their work sites, and caps off each evening with a program that helps them debrief their day and set it in the context of our Christian vocation to serve our neighbors. Noble work, right?

Now it's time to ask some hard questions to the organization. How do you handle housing? How are your bathrooms and showers designed? If I have a transgender youth, where would they stay? How will they be treated by program staff? What if I have twelve transgender youth? What about gay youth? Bisexual? Lesbian? Youth with two moms or two dads? How are they going to be treated in the registration process? Where will they be housed? Will they be around people they know and trust, or will they be placed with strangers who will at best distrust them and at worst harass them?

What about work assignments? Are only boys allowed to do construction work and girls relegated to packing food and reading to children? If part of the assignment is working with children, will LGBTQ youth or adult volunteers be prevented from volunteering? Will LGBTQ youth be allowed to talk honestly about their lives with their covolunteers and the people they are serving? If they are asked about dating, can they safely talk about their significant other on work sites?

If there is a large group program at the end of each day, what theology will ground the presentation? Who will be leading or preaching? What is their theology, and is it sufficiently compatible with ours that I want my youth exposed to it? What have the program's leaders said about LGBTQ people in the past? Will LGBTQ people be condemned explicitly in a message, sermon, or devotion?

Underlying all these questions is our main concern: "Will LGBTQ youth feel safe and be safe participating in your program?" There is power in asking these questions. Underpinning much of the anti-LGBTQ theology is the assumption that LGBTQ people and Christians are two separate communities, that there is no overlap, and that the two exist in opposition to each other. If you do not ask your questions, then no one will ever challenge that separatist and often homophobic worldview. The program organizers need to know that the vocal anti-LGBTQ churches are not the only ones who want to use their programming.

Be warned: in response to your questions, you might get some highly generalized answers. "We welcome everybody" can be an easy way for program representatives to avoid a difficult conversation. That's why it's so important to be very specific in your questioning. "We welcome everybody" might mean nothing more than "We will take your money." It doesn't guarantee that your youth will feel safe, much less affirmed. It doesn't mean that gender-binary stereotypes won't be reinforced. It doesn't mean that youth won't be forced into shared sleeping arrangements with a gender with which they don't identify and strangers, making them feel uncomfortable. So for the sake of your youth, have the courage to keep asking about specifics, thinking of every possible scenario where danger lurks for LGBTQ youth. The parachurch ministry probably hasn't read this book yet, and they aren't thinking through all the issues and questions that I'm lifting up on these pages. You will likely have to be the one who educates them. Do it for your youth.

The other set of questions has to do with the affiliations of the organization for which you are working—in our example, the one supporting the relief efforts. Make a list of these questions now, before you find yourself facing a decision about working with a particular organization. Does any portion of your fees go into any programs or campaigns that are working to diminish legal protections for LGBTQ people? Has the organization supported anti-LGBTQ bills in congress or in state legislatures (or their equivalent if in another country)? Have the organization's leaders or staff been associating with high-profile anti-LGBTQ leaders?[1] In short, you should ask yourself, Will our support of this ministry/work directly or indirectly fund the harm of the LGBTQ youth our church or organization is trying to support?

In the process of asking these hard questions, you might realize that the program is not a safe place for your youth. Then you will have to make the hard decision not to use that program. I don't underestimate how difficult this is. It means you are choosing to forego the convenience of having someone else take care of logistics for you. It means that your youth may not have access to the events that can mimic a rock concert. It means that you have just created more work for yourself to make an experience that is going to be edifying, formational, and fun for your youth.

But for the good of all LGBTQ people, including the youth you serve, I implore you to make the hard decision. Our society cannot change without churches and youth ministries challenging the status quo and proposing new ways to do ministry that can protect and honor who God made LGBTQ youth to be. We need you to be vocal so that we don't face the wall of exclusion when we step outside of your church.

You might think that what I'm asking for is overkill. You've perhaps rolled your eyes at the LGBTQ culture war fights over Chick-fil-A, *Duck Dynasty*, and the Salvation Army. Outside of The Naming Project, I work for the LGBTQ advocacy organization GLAAD. We've been in the middle of all three of those fights. I know firsthand that those who oppose the reality and existence of LGBTQ people are not just rolling their eyes and sitting back. They are calling our office to leave harassing voice-mail messages. They are contacting their businesses or branches to admonish them to continue to oppose LGBTQ people. They are not letting up, and they are policing the people and institutions in their own sphere of influence.

In 2014, news leaked that the Christian humanitarian organization World Vision was exploring the possibility of employing people in same-sex marriages. As soon as the news broke, anti-LGBTQ Christian leaders convinced their followers to end their support of the organization. The World Vision sponsorships of 3,500 poor children were immediately canceled.[2] Within two days, World Vision felt enough pressure to reverse their decision and announced that, once again, they would refuse to hire people in same-sex marriages, and presumably other members of the LGBTQ community.[3]

People invested in keeping LGBTQ people out of Christianity, its churches, and the organizations that support it are actively pushing for such harsh policies. Such advocacy is extremely vocal and intent on drowning out the faithful voices of LGBTQ inclusion. It is constant, and there is almost no opposition to it. Faithful Christians unwittingly go along with it because the convenience of handing off aspects of the ministry to another organization makes our lives as youth ministers a little easier.

Yes, saying no to or having to end your relationship with such convenient, fun, and slick organizations is going to mean more struggle for you. However, having your LGBTQ youth feel protected will more than make up for it.

CHAPTER
24

WHAT HAPPENS TO LGBTQ YOUTH OUTSIDE MY YOUTH GROUP?

Let's assume you've made your youth ministry and your church a safe and affirming place for LGBTQ youth. Let's assume you're even doing your best to ensure that any other ministry organizations with whom they come into contact are also safe places. In many ways, you may be an oasis in an otherwise hostile world for LGBTQ youth. But there is more to do.

Back in chapter 4, I described LGBTQ youth ministry as a series of concentric circles that start with self-affirmation as a beloved child of God, then move out to relationships, and end with justice for the wider world. Your youth ministry needs to be the same thing. It's a good start to make it a place where youth feel comfortable inside the walls of your church. But it's not enough. Our calling as Christians is to transform the world through the work of the gospel, not just our youth group.

From an LGBTQ perspective, the transformation of the world is public advocacy. It means preaching about the danger of anti-LGBTQ bills and the need for protections for LGBTQ youth. It means speaking publicly about the need for a ban on attempts to change sexual orientation and gender identity in youth. Thankfully, in recent years, legal bans on so-called conversion therapy for minors have been passed in several states, and we need Christian churches and youth ministers to support such bans loudly and publicly.

Yet at the same time, various states are passing or attempting to pass laws that target and police transgender youth. Beginning in 2019, laws have been passed in several states that give state legislatures the power to decide when and how transgender youth can participate in high school athletics.

As I was writing this chapter, Idaho's governor signed two antitransgender bills into law. One bans making gender changes on birth certificates. The other targets LGBTQ (especially transgender) youth in athletics, which is why I want to focus on it. It not only bars transgender youth from competing on the team that matches their gender identity but also opens the door for public accusations of any athlete's gender, possibly requiring them to undergo an invasive examination to "prove" their gender.[1]

Idaho isn't alone. In the 2020 legislative session, similar antitransgender youth athlete bills appeared in a dozen other states. Other bills being proposed include making it a felony for a doctor to provide transition-related care to LGBTQ youth. Some bills require states to report the parents of transgender youth to Child Protective Services—as if it were child abuse.[2]

Bills and laws like this are designed to punish those who love and support transgender youth. The proposed laws go against the standards of the American Medical Association and the recommendation of all professional care organizations. Simply caring for and supporting LGBTQ youth is being made into a criminal act. If parents and doctors of LGBTQ youth are being singled out and punished in this way, there is no reason that churches cannot be targeted for accepting and supporting youth as well.

These bills are not being introduced in a vacuum. The conditions are ripe for them to appear and be passed because loud voices are drowning out the expertise of doctors, counselors, teachers, and social workers and are instilling fear, confusion, and distrust about LGBTQ youth, especially transgender youth. Those who are leading the charge are claiming their activism is rooted in

Christian beliefs, even while they attempt to impose a rigid "either/or" binary gender structure on the world.

At such a time as this, your voice as a Christian minister is needed to change society so that your LGBTQ youth can be safe when they leave the walls of their church. They need to be safe enough at school to receive an education, which in turn will propel them into responsible adulthood and make them faithful, empathetic, and healthy members of society.

Jesus's Great Commission at the end of Matthew's Gospel exhorts us to make disciples of all nations. Such discipleship is ultimately about the transformation of the world. Your youth ministry won't transform the world unless you bring your love, support, and acceptance outside the walls of the church.

This responsibility does not have to fall to you alone, but your leadership will be necessary. Your youth can be empowered to speak up, to tell their story of coming out or their journey to allyship. Parents can talk about wanting a world that is safe for their children and what laws and cultural norms are going to be necessary to make the world a safe place for them. Pastors can infuse their messages with rich, life-generating theology. And everyone can invoke their most meaningful passage of Scripture to drive the point home that they are not speaking merely for themselves but are doing their part to fulfill Jesus's call to transform the world.

Your church doesn't have to do it alone. Resources like LGBTQ advocacy groups now welcome both youth and faith leader participation. You can get involved in local or state-level organizing, adding a Christian lens to the advocacy happening through statewide LGBTQ organizations. A church outing to a lobbying day or rally is both an educational and empowering process for all involved. Here's how:

Imagine that your statewide LGBTQ organization is having a rally in support of nondiscrimination measures. First, spend time in study and prayer. Talk about what you value as a congregation and as a youth group. Look up stories of discrimination in the Bible. Learn who is protected by nondiscrimination laws and who is left out. Then you can decide as a youth group or congregation if and how you will participate in the rally.

But your prework isn't done yet. Spend time planning your church presence. Make sure others at the rally know that you are Christians supporting nondiscrimination protections for LGBTQ people. How? Perhaps spend time making signs in the youth room, letting individual youth identify a Bible passage that supports nondiscrimination. Plan to wear congregational shirts to the rally.

Then once you're at the rally itself, listen closely to the speakers and for statements of faith and values. When the rally is over, debrief with the youth. Ask, What was empowering? What was difficult? Why might someone resist nondiscrimination? What arguments might change their hearts?

This process doesn't have to be "political," but it should be a way to live out your values.

You will likely find that some youth have an interest and aptitude for LGBTQ advocacy. Encourage youth who demonstrate leadership potential and have an interest in advocacy to attend LGBTQ youth leadership conferences, which will equip them with the skills to articulate their faith in a meaningful way. Take a look at the list of organizations with youth and faith programs in appendix B and add your own organizations to the list. Consider a preference for organizations that are led by people of color, transgender people, and those who have often been marginalized in both the church and the secular LGBTQ movement.

Such activity can feel like a departure from what "youth ministry" is meant to be. But advocacy is a continued form to live out Jesus's Great Commission. If your congregation is the only safe place around, youth will still be living in a dangerous world. We cannot guarantee their safety, but we can promise to equip them to navigate the world. We can walk with them for the long haul. We can pray for them daily.

Beyond praying for our youth, we can pray that the world will become a place that welcomes, loves, accepts, and celebrates youth as the complex, divinely created beings they are. But when we pray for such a change, we have to be open to the possibility that we are the ones who can create a better, more inclusive place for LGBTQ youth. We may be called to be the very advocates for whom we are praying.

As a youth minister and an LGBTQ advocate, my two worlds often reinforce one another in just such a way. I am motivated to be an LGBTQ advocate because I want to make a better world for the youth to whom I minister. I minister because I want to build up the leaders who are going to help me create that better world. It's the calling I've received from God. I've said, "Here I am, Lord." And I've been blessed for doing so. I think you'll find the same.

CHAPTER

25

NOW WHAT?

Now that you've reached the end of the book, you may have far more questions than you had at the beginning. That's OK. There will always be more questions. The LGBTQ community is continuously evolving. The issues that define me as a white, fortysomething-year-old, cisgender man and my generation are not the same issues that LGBTQ youth are facing today. New terms to describe identity will continue to crop up as portions of the community that we've overlooked or actively erased assert their identity.

And who will lead all these changes? Youth.

Youth ministry is a nurturing role, one that teaches and helps shape faithful Christian adults. But we learn and grow so much as adults by watching, listening, and learning from the young people in our churches. Yes, we will be helping them grow in Christ, but they will also be helping us grow.

We grow as we learn from others and also as we make things up on the spot. That's OK. That's what I did. That's what all the founders of The Naming Project did. We didn't set out to create an LGBTQ youth ministry. We saw a need, and we tried to figure out what we could do to fill that need. We tried something, evaluated, changed things, and tried again.

Making things up is what we continue to do now, years later. Every time we meet new LGBTQ youth, an unexpected issue challenges us: mental illness, physical injury, self-harm, couples in our youth group, manipulation, oversexualized jokes, racism, and so on.

Not all the issues are heavy. We've heard novel, imaginative interpretations of Scripture. We've laughed uproariously at jokes and gasped at the sheer talent our youth display. We've witnessed mutual support and care. We've been a part of challenging prejudices and watched biases fall. We've seen unconditional love. And we've been surprised.

Initially, I hadn't paid much attention to Fiona. She was one of the youngest youth in our group and also an introvert who spoke up only when she felt it was necessary. But when she did speak up, some of the most profound questions and statements came from her. All the counselors were astonished at the thought and maturity of her contributions. And just when our awe of this prodigy was at its peak, she walked into a screen door carrying a plate of food. It was a humorous reminder that our campers are complex figures, capable of greatness and folly all at once.

Like many of you, I think of the youth who have been in my ministry as "my" kids. I care about them, want to nurture them, want them to succeed, and want to shield them from trouble. But we cannot protect LGBTQ youth in every situation. Even if they find our youth groups to be safe places, they will still experience rejection, bullying, and discrimination. I wish it weren't true, but we live in a broken, sinful world in which some LGBTQ youth will continue to be rejected by peers, by family, by schools, and by society. The more you know this reality, the more you can prepare yourself and your youth to handle rejection and adversity. And you continually pray that they will overcome challenges and become smarter and more resilient with each victory.

Eventually, your LGBTQ youth will graduate and cease to be youth. They will move on to other pursuits in other communities: college, work, the military, and families of their own. And as they do, you will continue to pray that they will be healthy adults, rooted and grounded in God's love wherever they go. That's how we pass on this ministry to the next generation that will use in turn their skills and gifts for the good of the world.

I hope that one day, one of The Naming Project youth will become a leader in the church, a pastor or a deacon, spreading the gospel through a formal church structure and being called and paid to do just that. Since the calling to ministry comes from God, it's not something I, or any of the adult leaders, can force. Instead, I try to make sure that I name the gifts for ministry that I see in our youth. It may be eloquent speaking, a deep empathy, and an interest in Scripture or theology. Even if they don't go onto seminary and become ordained ministers or deacons like me, I want them to recognize those gifts in themselves and become laypersons empowered to share the gospel in whatever setting they are in.

For many, that calling may not be in a formal church setting. Some of our campers have followed up their time at The Naming Project with internships at LGBTQ advocacy organizations, in marriage-equality campaigns, in an LGBTQ health care setting, or in state and local service organizations. Our alumni take seriously the issues the LGBTQ community still faces today, and they are finding specific ways to help.

I've encouraged several of our youth to apply for an internship at GLAAD, where I work as a program director. A few have done so. One is subsequently working in LGBTQ health care. His passion for helping people and the support he had during the medical portion of his transition meant that he wanted to give back in some way.

Another youth developed an interest in drag from a fellow youth at our summer camp. They went home and continued to perform drag, becoming a local celebrity and a significant fundraiser for charities. Through it all, they continue to volunteer for church youth gatherings, supporting other young people who are growing up and discovering and nurturing their own faith.

Other alumni have gone into the arts. One has toured the country with *Hamilton*, while another is a staple of the Twin Cities musical theater scene. Jacob, a five-time camper from Georgia, was obsessed with Broadway and was usually the third-base coach during our games of show tunes kickball, teaching songs to campers who weren't into musical theater as much as he was. He blasted show tunes from a portable speaker during our arts and crafts sessions and would talk about Broadway with anyone who would listen.

After attending The Naming Project for several years, Jacob went to college in Atlanta and started working in the theater. When I was organizing a GLAAD bus tour across the US South, I reached out to Jacob and found that he was involved in a youth theater company doing a production of *Bare: A Pop Opera*, a musical that deals with issues of religion, sexuality, and identity, the same themes we had been building at The Naming Project for so many years. I arranged for some GLAAD staff to attend the production and participate in a talkback after the show. During the talkback, Jacob shared his experience attending The Naming Project. He was accepted by his parents and his church. The Naming Project added faithful peers who helped him grow into a well-adjusted adult, assured that God loved him and secure enough to share that message with others through words and actions. He also said that he wanted to use the arts to share that message and that shows like *Bare: A Pop Opera* are helping him do that.

Some of our alumni work in corporate America. Some are married and have kids of their own, while others are single. Some are successful by worldly standards, while all of them—like us—struggle with the ongoing challenges of life.

But the LGBTQ youth's value lies not in what they do but in them living fully as God created them. That, after all, is the mission of The Naming Project. We remind our youth that despite the names or labels the world gives them—birth names that do not fit, unwanted nicknames branded by bullies, titles they achieve, or slurs hurled at them—God knows each one of them by name.

How does God know us so intimately? Because God created us. This creation isn't a "mass production" but rather an intimate, careful, handcrafted relationship. And because God created us, God knows us deeply and intimately. God knows us better than we know ourselves. During adolescence, we are figuring out who we are, but God already knows us . . . even as we are discovering ourselves. And because God made and knows us, God loves us. Deeply.

Though the world often tells us that we cannot be more than one thing at a time, that's simply not true. We are people who have multiple parts of our identity. As one of our adult leaders, Pastor Megan, told the campers during an evening worship, "God wants you to be the you-iest you possible." That phrase recognizes that we are created with an infinite combination of skills, quirks, fears, desires, dreams, and attributes. We are not just our sexual orientation or gender identity any more than we are just our race or ability. It is only by understanding that God made us to be whole people that we can do real, authentic ministry with youth.

Psalm 139 speaks directly of God's intimate knowledge about us. It is a helpful reminder for all of us who are told that we don't fit in because of who we are. It counters the notion that we are "weird" or that God's creation cannot include some aspect of our identity. It underlies how I think of myself as a gay Christian. It speaks not just of my value but of the careful crafting that has gone into every member of this big, broad LGBTQ community:

> O Lord, you have searched me and known me.
> You know when I sit down and when I rise up; you discern my
>   thoughts from far away.
> You search out my path and my lying down, and are acquainted
>   with all my ways.
> Even before a word is on my tongue, O Lord, you know it
>   completely.
> You hem me in, behind and before, and lay your hand upon me.
> Such knowledge is too wonderful for me; it is so high that I cannot
>   attain it.
> Where can I go from your spirit? Or where can I flee from your
>   presence?
> If I ascend to heaven, you are there; if I make my bed in Sheol, you
>   are there.

If I take the wings of the morning and settle at the farthest limits of
the sea,

even there your hand shall lead me, and your right hand shall hold
me fast.

If I say, "Surely the darkness shall cover me, and the light around me
become night,"

even the darkness is not dark to you; the night is as bright as the day,
for darkness is as light to you.

For it was you who formed my inward parts; you knit me together in
my mother's womb.

I praise you, for I am fearfully and wonderfully made. Wonderful are
your works; that I know very well.

My frame was not hidden from you, when I was being made in
secret, intricately woven in the depths of the earth.

Your eyes beheld my unformed substance. In your book were
written all the days that were formed for me, when none of
them as yet existed.

How weighty to me are your thoughts, O God! How vast is the sum
of them!

I try to count them—they are more than the sand; I come to the
end—I am still with you.

O that you would kill the wicked, O God, and that the bloodthirsty
would depart from me—

those who speak of you maliciously, and lift themselves up against
you for evil!

Do I not hate those who hate you, O Lord? And do I not loathe
those who rise up against you?

I hate them with perfect hatred; I count them my enemies.

Search me, O God, and know my heart; test me and know my
thoughts.

See if there is any wicked way in me, and lead me in the way
   everlasting.[1]

All the aspects of our identities come from God, and they all tumble and
realign and reform constantly throughout our lives to make me and you so
we can hear and understand and believe it when we are told that God wants
us to be the "you-iest you" possible. You, the work of God's hand. You, the
created being, with a variety of gifts and faults. You, the beloved child of God.

Numerically, The Naming Project youth ministry is small—as your
LGBTQ ministry likely is or will be too. Our summer camp averages fifteen
youth. But the assurance that our LGBTQ and allied youth are created in the
image of God, known by God and loved by God, influences every interaction
they have. It grounds them and makes them an influence on their friends,
family, coworkers, and even strangers. Thanks to this knowledge, they may
be able to handle a moment of injustice a little stronger. They may be able to
provide comfort to someone in their time of need. They may hear a passage of
Scripture and be transported back to when we talked about that Scripture in
our morning Bible study.

Because we are made, because we are known, God is with us. We are
called precious and honored. We need not fear the names we may be given in
this world. We can trust that God's name for us—"child of God"—will leave
a lasting impression. Perhaps the most important aspect of your work with
LGBTQ youth will be this: to remind them that they are each a child of God,
fully known, loved, and valued.

APPENDIX A

RESOURCES ON THE CHRISTIAN ARGUMENT FOR LGBTQ EQUALITY AND ACCEPTANCE

While this book assumes you want to minister effectively with LGBTQ youth, not everyone has been convinced that ministry with LGBTQ people is faithful or prudent. Some may want to minister *to* LGBTQ people without the possibility of being the *recipients of* ministry from this population. Others may want to exclude LGBTQ people from churches completely.

Others will be more conflicted. They are good people and want to do the right thing, but they honestly don't know what the right thing is. They have probably been raised with a worldview that associates LGBTQ people with sin. They may have heard only negative stories about LGBTQ people. But they are open to learning more.

The approach for each person is going to be different, and this makes recommending resources difficult. The following is a list of books that approach the intersection of LGBTQ people and Christianity differently. If you already know those with whom you are dealing, you can match the approach that fits their learning ability, their worldview, and their values.

The Naming Project

While most of this book has been about what we have learned through developing and running The Naming Project, it remains a valuable resource for you as a Christian adult working with LGBTQ youth or for the youth themselves.

The Naming Project continues to operate its summer camp program. We continue to evolve our ministry in response to a changing world and find ways to connect with youth, parents, pastors, youth ministers, and adult volunteers who care about the well-being of LGBTQ youth. Our focus is on youth ministry, and we have expanded our offerings to include regular virtual campfires, reflections, and partnerships with other inclusive youth ministries.

The leaders of The Naming Project are available for consultation on how to integrate the best practices of youth ministry LGBTQ with your particular context.

Learn more at www.thenamingproject.org.

Biblical and Theological Research with a Personal Touch

Changing Our Mind: The Landmark Call for Inclusion of LGBTQ Christians with Response to Critics (Read the Spirit Books)
Describing LGBTQ people as a "hot-button issue," theologian David P. Gushee takes the reader along on his personal and theological journey as he examines his previous assumptions and eventually changes his mind about gay, lesbian, bisexual, and transgender inclusion in the Church.

God and the Gay Christian: The Biblical Case in Support of Same-Sex Relationships (Convergent Books)
Matthew Vines takes people through the biblical argument that helped him make the Christian case for LGBTQ inclusion. Part memoir, he focuses on convincing his family and his conservative hometown that his being gay was not inherently sinful. This book is helpful for those who see the Bible as the biggest source of opposition to LGBTQ welcome and inclusion.

The Gospel of Inclusion: A Christian Case for LGBT+ Inclusion in the Church (Cascade Books)
Evangelical pastor and public theologian Brandan Robertson offers an assessment of biblical texts, cultural context, and modern social movements to suggest that the entire Christian gospel calls the church to create a world that

celebrates the full spectrum of human diversity, including LGBTQ people, as a reflection of God's creative intention.

Walking the Bridgeless Canyon: Repairing the Breach between the Church and the LGBT Community (Canyonwalker Press)
Kathy Baldock is a straight evangelical Christian who researched the historical, cultural, medical, and political filters of discrimination through which the LGBTQ community is seen. Baldock constructs a timeline of various religious influences to understand the current evangelical view of LGBTQ people, including an examination of what the Bible says about same-sex behavior. The book also offers the resources and tools needed to make informed and wise, Christ-centered choices when interacting with LGBTQ people and their detractors.

Handbooks and Guides for Living as a Faithful LGBTQ Child of God

Bulletproof Faith: A Spiritual Survival Guide for Gay and Lesbian Christians (Jossey-Bass)
The Reverend Candace Chellew-Hodge's practical guide shows readers a way through the minefield of condemnation and persecution that LGBTQ Christians face and helps foster a faith that is bulletproof—impervious to attacks yet loving and savvy in its approach. Chellew-Hodge teaches spiritual practices that deflect attacks and enhance and strengthen faith by turning attacks into opportunities for spiritual growth.

Queerfully and Wonderfully Made: A Guide for LGBTQ+ Christian Teens (Beaming Books)
This handbook is designed to speak directly to youth, answering questions they have about growing up and navigating the world as an LGBTQ Christian. It begins by addressing the question about whether there is something wrong with LGBTQ youth and answers with an unequivocal *no!* This is less about making the case about LGBTQ youth than about helping LGBTQ Christian youth live as fully and authentically as possible.

Transforming: The Bible and the Lives of Transgender Christians (Westminster John Knox Press)

Austen Hartke offers a biblically based, educational, and affirming resource to shed light and wisdom on the transgender experience and the gender landscape. He does this by introducing transgender issues and language and providing stories of both biblical characters and real-life narratives from transgender Christians living today.

Welcoming and Affirming: A Guide to Supporting and Working with LGBTQ+ Christian Youth (Broadleaf Books)

A companion to *Queerfully and Wonderfully Made*, this handbook is for the adults working with LGBTQ youth in ministry settings. As it answers questions about best supporting LGBTQ youth, the book features personal testimonies that address the joys and challenges of living as LGBTQ Christians.

Memoirs with Something to Teach

Facing the Music: My Story (Howard Books)

Jennifer Knapp tells the story of her childhood, falling deeply in love with both music and Christianity, and her meteoric rise to stardom in the Christian contemporary music scene. The tension she felt between her public persona and her understanding of her personal identity caused an abrupt departure from the Christian music industry. After coming to terms with her sexual orientation, Knapp returned to music and came out publicly. Despite the many who claim she can no longer call herself a believer, she maintains that she is both gay and a Christian.

A Life of Unlearning—a Preacher's Struggle with His Homosexuality, Church and Faith (Personal Success Australia)

Anthony Venn-Brown tells his story of being a popular Pentecostal preacher while realizing he was gay. Believing that his homosexuality made him unacceptable to God and others, Venn-Brown underwent a twenty-two-year period of prayer, struggle, torment, gay conversion therapy, and marriage. After Venn-Brown came out, he was abandoned by his church and Christian friends. And so began his life of unlearning—a lonely journey that made him the Christian leader he is today.

One Coin Found: How God's Love Stretches to the Margins (Fortress Press)
The Reverend Emmy Kegler is a queer woman who grew up in both conservative Evangelical and progressive Protestant churches. She understood how Scripture can wound and exclude, but it continued to captivate and inspire her. She set out on a journey to fall in love with the Bible, wrestling with its stories. In her study of the Bible, she found that God's story is a story of welcome and acceptance for everyone—no exceptions.

Torn: Rescuing the Gospel from the Gays-vs.-Christians Debate (Jericho Books)
This memoir follows the life of Justin Lee, a deeply devout Baptist who wore his faith identity on his sleeve and also knew he was gay. Having been told that being gay and Christian were in opposition, Lee first hid the truth, then tried to eradicate the gay part of himself. Only through a journey of Scripture study and self-examination was he able to come to a place of self-acceptance. Lee went on to found an online and in-person community for others who were feeling the same conflict he felt.

Unashamed: A Coming Out Guide for LGBTQ Christians (Westminster John Knox Press)
Amber Cantorna, the gay daughter of a thirty-plus-year executive of conservative Christian organization Focus on the Family, tells her personal story of coming out to her family and how that journey went from losing everything to fulfillment and wisdom to share. She uses her story as a guide for Christians considering coming out, tackling tough subject matters such as demolishing internalized homophobia, finding an affirming faith community, reestablishing your worth as a child of God, navigating difficult family conversations, and healing from the pain of rejection.

Undivided: Coming Out, Becoming Whole, and Living Free from Shame (HarperOne)

Vicky Beeching chronicles her career in the Christian music industry and her decision to come out as gay—a decision that led to self-acceptance and acknowledgment, which in turn changed her relationship with God and the practice of her faith. For ten years, Vicky rejected who she really was—a denial that damaged her in body and soul. Vicky discovered that she could not worship God with a pure heart if she did not accept who she was. When she came out publicly in 2014, Vicky lost the support of her Christian community. But she gained much more: the truth had set her free.

APPENDIX B

LGBTQ CHRISTIAN ORGANIZATIONS

While you are building LGBTQ competency in your youth ministry, you may feel some isolation. You may feel as if you are the only one in your church or your denomination who is thinking about the youth ministry implications of LGBTQ Christians. Or perhaps you want to use resources specific to your tradition to address LGBTQ inclusion in a much more theologically nuanced way.

For several years, I was fortunate to work with The Institute for Welcoming Resources, a faith-specific arm of the National LGBTQ Task Force. The institute partnered with several LGBTQ organizations working in mainline Protestant denominations to provide LGBTQ-specific resources, provide Building an Inclusive Church training, and create a network of best practices to help lift all boats.

Most of the following descriptions of the mainline Protestant denominations are adapted from the Institute for Welcoming Resources website.[1] I have also worked with Catholic, Evangelical, and other denominations and felt it was important to include them in this list. Their descriptions are adapted from the organizational websites, listed with the title.

Of course, there are many other LGBTQ Christian organizations and several for other world religions. Some are support groups, some are advocacy groups, and some are both. Many host events for people to gather physically, while others exist only virtually through a website or on social media.

It is always worth a look to see who is doing creative work around LGBTQ inclusion. For example, the New Jersey Synod of the Evangelical Lutheran Church in America hosted an event titled "Faith, Hope & Love: Building Safer and More Welcoming Congregations for LGBTQ+ Youth."[2] The synod-sponsored event was designed for youth, pastors, and youth ministers, with resources available for each. The organizers invited both secular and religious programs to provide resources and present workshops. The daylong event was bookended with a large gathering to set the tone and a closing worship, complete with Holy Communion.

Events and gatherings like this are happening in large and small settings, organized both formally and informally. I cannot name everything happening out there, but the list below is designed to point you to some of the best places to start your search.

Denominationally Affiliated Independent Organizations
The organizations in this section are independent from the denominations and church bodies to which they are advocating. These organizations understand the polity and culture of their specific faith tradition and often collaborate on faith issues impacting wider society.

Affirmation: LGBTQ Mormons, Families & Friends
Church of Jesus Christ of Latter-day Saints
www.affirmation.org

Affirm United / S'affirmer Ensemble
United Church of Canada
www.ause.ca

The Association of Welcoming & Affirming Baptists
American Baptists USA, Alliance of Baptists, and others
www.awab.org

Brethren Mennonite Council for LGBT Interest
Mennonite and Church of the Brethren communities
www.bmclgbt.org

DignityUSA
Roman Catholic
www.dignityusa.org

Disciples LGBTQ+ Alliance
The Christian Church (Disciples of Christ)
www.disciplesallianceq.org

The Evangelical Network
Evangelical
www.ten.lgbt

Extraordinary Lutheran Ministries
Lutheran
www.elm.org

The Fellowship of Affirming Ministries
African American Christian leadership
www.radicallyinclusive.org

Integrity
The Episcopal Church
www.integritylistensandspeaks.org

Many Voices
Black church
www.manyvoices.org

More Light Presbyterians
Presbyterian Church (USA)
www.mlp.org

New Ways Ministry
Catholic
www.newwaysministry.org

Q Christian Fellowship
Pan-Christian
www.qchristian.org

Reconciling Ministries Network
The United Methodist Church
www.rmnetwork.org

ReconcilingWorks: Lutherans for Full Participation
Lutheran
www.reconcilingworks.org

Room for All
Reformed Church in America
www.roomforall.com

Seventh-day Adventist Kinship International
Seventh-day Adventist
www.sdakinship.org

Soulforce
Pan-Christian
www.soulforce.org

Welcoming Community Network
Community of Christ
www.welcomingcommunitynetwork.org

LGBTQ Denominations
The denominations listed in this section either have been created for the purpose of ministering to the LGBTQ community or has created programming within the denominational structure for LGBTQ people.

Metropolitan Community Church
www.mccchurch.org

Open and Affirming Coalition of the United Church of Christ
www.openandaffirming.org

Unitarian Universalist Association
www.uua.org

APPENDIX C

LGBTQ HOLY DAYS FOR YOUR YOUTH MINISTRY TO COMMEMORATE

During a group meeting, a youth ministry friend of mine shared her personal pet peeve. "Why do churches align themselves with the academic calendar?" she ranted. "We have a liturgical calendar, and I don't see why I have to give that up just because it's summer vacation or prom season or homecoming."

She had a point, but she was also used to integrating the liturgical calendar, with its ritualized history of Jesus's life, death, and resurrection as well as points of celebration and contemplation, with the cycle of the academic calendar, creating new beginnings, short and long breaks, seasons, and celebrations of its own. In the United States, our youth ministry programs have all melded the liturgical and school calendars, holding "Senior Sunday" for graduating congregational members and "Rally Sunday" with the launch of the school year and changing summer programming to involve more trips and camps.

If we can include all those into our academic-year youth ministry planning, then surely we can also be aware of some of the LGBTQ holy days. Some of those holy days may provide inspiration for Bible studies, activities, themed worship, or community engagement. Others may at least raise our awareness and bring a sense of community to a youth who shares any of the identities listed in the holy days.

The list below is some of the most common LGBTQ commemoration days. The list is likely not exhaustive, as expanding identities continue to develop new awareness every day. Besides the following list, check with your local LGBTQ organizations to see if there are any state- or local-specific commemorations or historical markers. For example, even though June is typically considered Pride Month, many places celebrate it at different times in the year. In many southern states, Pride is celebrated in October, simply because cooler temperatures make for more pleasant parades.

Many of the dates listed below are related to HIV and AIDS commemoration days, often with specific targeted communities.[1] The reason HIV is often closely associated with the LGBTQ community is that when it was first discovered (but not yet fully understood), it was named GRID—gay-related immune deficiency. However, AIDS impacts persons of every sexual orientation, gender identity, and race. The various awareness days are designed to share information specific to each identity. The overarching themes of each of these days are prevention, testing, treatment, the end of stigma around HIV, and the call for a vaccine.

FEBRUARY

February 7 **National Black HIV/AIDS Awareness Day** increases HIV education, testing, community involvement, and treatment among Black communities.

MARCH

March 10 **National Women and Girls HIV/AIDS Awareness Day** is a day to learn more about the impact of HIV and AIDS on women and girls.

March 20 **National Native HIV/AIDS Awareness Day** is recognized on the first day of spring to draw attention to the impact of HIV on indigenous communities as well as to call for access to testing and treatment.

March 31 **International Transgender Day of Visibility** shows support for the transgender community by spreading knowledge and awareness of the transgender community and its various members around the world.

APRIL

April 10   **National Youth HIV and AIDS Awareness Day** focuses on the impact of HIV/AIDS on youth and highlights the work youth lead in the fight against AIDS.

April 18   **National Transgender HIV Testing Day** recognizes the importance of routine HIV testing, status awareness, and continued focus on HIV prevention and treatment efforts among transgender and gender nonbinary people.

April 26   **Lesbian Visibility Day** is a visibility campaign to publically identify yourself as a lesbian or support the lesbians in your life.

Late April (day varies from year to year)   **Day of Silence** is a student-led national event that brings attention to anti-LGBTQ name-calling, bullying, and harassment in schools. Students take a vow of silence in an effort to encourage schools and classmates to address the problem of anti-LGBTQ behavior by illustrating the silencing effect of bullying and harassment on LGBTQ students and those perceived to be LGBTQ.

MAY

May 17   **International Day against Homophobia, Transphobia, and Biphobia** celebrates the anniversary of the day in 1990 when the World Health Organization removed the classification of homosexuality as a disease. The day draws attention to the situation faced by LGBTQ people around the world.

May 18   **HIV Vaccine Awareness Day** commemorates the volunteers, community members, health professionals, and scientists working together to find a safe and effective preventive HIV vaccine as well as to educate about the importance of HIV vaccine research.

May 19   **National Asian and Pacific Islander HIV/AIDS Awareness Day** is a national campaign to end silence and shame about HIV/AIDS in Asian and Pacific Islander communities.

May 24   **Pansexual and Panromantic Awareness and Visibility Day** celebrates the pansexual and panromantic community and educates others about the community.

JUNE

LGBTQ Pride Month is celebrated in the United States and many places around the world in June in honor of the Stonewall riots, though Pride events occur throughout the year. June has also been when major LGBTQ advancements were made through the Supreme Court, including decriminalization of same-sex relationships in 2003 and marriage equality in 2015.

June 5   **HIV Long-Term Survivors Day** celebrates and honors long-term survivors of the epidemic and raises awareness of their needs, issues, and journeys.

June 12   The **Pulse Remembrance** honors the forty-nine LGBTQ and allied people murdered at the Pulse nightclub in Orlando, Florida, in 2016.

June 27   **National HIV Testing Day** encourages people to get tested for HIV, know their status, and get linked to care and treatment.

June 28   The **Stonewall Riots Anniversary** date is what kicked off the modern LGBTQ movement.

JULY

July 14   **International Nonbinary People's Day** was chosen to fall between International Men's Day and International Women's Day to raise awareness of nonbinary people.

SEPTEMBER

September 18   **National HIV/AIDS and Aging Awareness Day** brings attention to the growing number of people living long and full lives with HIV and to their health and social needs.

September 16–23   **Bisexual Awareness Week** celebrates and raises accurate awareness of the bisexual community. The week caps off with **Celebrate Bisexuality Day** on September 23.

September 27   **National Gay Men's HIV/AIDS Awareness Day** recognizes the disproportionate impact of the epidemic on gay men.

OCTOBER

LGBT History Month was first celebrated in 1994 and was subsequently declared a national history month for the United States by President Barack Obama in 2009 to encourage openness and education about LGBTQ history and rights.

October 11 **National Coming Out Day** celebrates LGBTQ people's coming out experiences and journeys.

October 15 **National Latinx AIDS Awareness Day** reaches Latinx/Hispanic communities to promote HIV testing and provide HIV prevention information and access to care.

Third Thursday in October **Spirit Day** is a day on which millions of people wear purple in a stand against bullying and to show their support for LGBTQ youth.

October 22–28 **Asexual Awareness Week** educates about asexual, aromantic, demisexual, and gray-asexual experiences and to create materials that are accessible to the asexual community and allies around the world.

October 26 **Intersex Awareness Day** commemorates the first public demonstration by intersex people in North America.

NOVEMBER

November 8 **Intersex Solidarity Day** is also known as **Intersex Day of Remembrance** and marks the birthday of Herculine Barbin, a now famous French intersex person.

November 20 **International Transgender Day of Remembrance** memorializes those who were killed due to antitransgender hatred or prejudice.

DECEMBER

December 1 **World AIDS Day** is an opportunity for people worldwide to unite in the fight against HIV, show their support for people living with HIV, and commemorate those who have died from AIDS.

APPENDIX D

OTHER HELPFUL RESOURCES

Believe Out Loud

www.believeoutloud.com

Believe Out Loud is a program created to encourage Christian clergy to voice their affirmation for LGBTQ people. Since its founding in 2008, Believe Out Loud has grown into an online and in-person community that creates space—literally, virtually, and spiritually—for LGBTQ people and their allies to live full, authentic, and free lives. Believe Out Loud launches campaigns on its website, on various social media platforms, and through workshops, seminars, and events to help people find community, information, and spiritual affirmation.[1]

Building an Inclusive Church

www.welcomingresources.org/welcomingtoolkit.pdf

Building an Inclusive Church is a training program for congregations that are considering whether to make a welcome statement that includes people of all sexual orientations and gender identities. More than just the requirements to qualify for rosters of welcoming and affirming congregation, both the training and the toolkit focus on faith-based community organizing. The program provides participants a realistic sense of how easy or difficult it is to become welcoming and affirming. They teach skills to understand what members of your congregation value and how to best talk to them about being welcoming and affirming.

This process is not specific to youth ministry, but the questions and the skills taught in the training will be just as useful for building an inclusive youth ministry as it will for other aspects of congregational life. In particular, the skills will also be applicable for public advocacy, internal decision-making, and becoming a leader in the community.

Music That Makes Community

www.musicthatmakescommunity.org

Music That Makes Community is an organization I highly recommend to help your youth ministry (or your entire congregation) move away from noninclusive Christian music. I had a few friends who were involved in the organization, but I hadn't paid much attention to it until The Naming Project had an adult volunteer leader who was involved in the organization and came prepared with songs that matched our theme, pulled from a variety of sources. The best part was that most songs have movement included. Nothing complicated, but rhythmic movements. Some songs are light and fun, some are contemplative. All of them are based on the assurance of God's love for creation.

I highly recommend looking into this resource for learning new songs, having a member teach music for an event, or shifting your entire repertoire to such resources. Their teaching is "paperless" and based on learning songs by heart rather than by text.[2]

Our Whole Lives

https://tinyurl.com/hdam36c

Our Whole Lives is a series of sexuality education programs. It is broken down into six age categories: grades K–1, grades 4–6, grades 7–9, grades 10–12, young adults, and adults. Published jointly by the United Church of Christ and the Unitarian Universalist Association, the curriculum was designed by professional sexuality educators to be used in churches and faith-based spaces, and yet the curriculum is inclusive of sexual orientations and gender identity.

As of this writing, The Naming Project leaders have been trained in the 10–12 grade program. We have found the curriculum to be age appropriate. It includes six subject areas: human development, relationships, personal skills, sexual behavior, sexual health, and society and culture. The curriculum includes accurate information about anatomy and human development but maintains a focus on values and interpersonal skills. Participants learn the social, emotional, and spiritual aspects of sexuality.[3]

Yass, Jesus!

www.yassjesuspod.com

Yass, Jesus! is a podcast that addresses Christianity from a distinctly queer perspective. Hosted by Daniel Franzese, an actor best known for *Mean Girls* and *Looking*, and Azariah Southworth, the former host of *The Remix* on TBN, this podcast explores Bible stories, Christian communities, and interviews with celebrities you didn't know were both queer and Christian.

NOTES

INTRODUCTION

1 Throughout this book, I use the acronym *LGBTQ*, which is most often broken down into "lesbian, gay, bisexual, transgender, and queer." However, there are variations to this acronym. In addition to "queer," the Q can also refer to "questioning." Other letters may also be included, depending on the community. In many international communities, *I* for "intersex" is included. And occasionally, *A* is added to refer to either "asexual" or occasionally "ally."

2 These are real questions that have been emailed to The Naming Project.

3 Soon Kyu Choi, Bianca D. M. Wilson, Jama Shelton, and Gary Gates, *Serving Our Youth 2015: The Needs and Experiences of Lesbian, Gay, Bisexual, Transgender, and Questioning Youth Experiencing Homelessness* (Los Angeles: The Palette Fund, True Colors Fund, The Williams Institute, 2015), https://truecolorsunited.org/servingouryouth.

4 In 2012, Lutherans Concerned / North America was rebranded as ReconcilingWorks. For clarity, I will consistently use ReconcilingWorks throughout this book.

5 See appendix B for a fuller list of LGBTQ Christian organizations.

CHAPTER 1: What Questions Should I Be Asking about LGBTQ Youth Ministry?

1 Ross Murray, Jay Wiesner, and Brad Froslee, "About The Naming Project," The Naming Project, 2015, accessed February 8, 2020. https://www.thenamingproject.org/about/.

2 Some youth names have been changed to protect their privacy.

CHAPTER 2: What If I Encounter Resistance Establishing an LGBTQ Youth Ministry?

1 "Reconciling in Christ (RIC)," ReconcilingWorks, accessed June 22, 2020, www.reconcilingworks.org/ric; "Open and Affirming in the UCC," United Church of Christ, accessed June 22, 2020, www.ucc.org/lgbt_ona.

2 Rebecca Voelkel, Vicki Wunsch, David Lohman, and Tim Feiertag, *Building an Inclusive Church: A Welcoming Toolkit 2.0: Helping Your Congregation Become a Community That Openly Welcomes People of All Sexual Orientations and Gender Identities*

(Washington, DC: National Gay and Lesbian Task Force's Institute for Welcoming Resources, 2013), https://tinyurl.com/y6s6l28y.

3 Anonymous, "Bp Johnson Risks Legal Exposure," *Lutheran Commentator* 18, no. 1 (July–September 2004): 4.

4 The Naming Project has had a long relationship with Bay Lake Camp in Deerwood, Minnesota. All our summer programming has been held there, and they have been a wonderful partner. Bay Lake Camp is owned by First Lutheran Church in St. Paul, Minnesota, and rents its facilities to any church, retreat, conference, and so on that wants to use it. They have participated in as much or as little of our programming as we've needed, www.baylakecamp.com.

CHAPTER 3: Should I Set Up a Program Exclusively for LGBTQ Youth? Or Just Practice Inclusivity?

1 One Million Moms is a program of the American Family Association. While their name implies a large and powerful organization, they have very few members. They are mostly known for complaining about LGBTQ-inclusive media, mostly under the guise of its being inappropriate for children; www.onemillionmoms.com.

2 Rebecca Voelkel, Vicki Wunsch, David Lohman, and Tim Feiertag, *Building an Inclusive Church: A Welcoming Toolkit 2.0: Helping Your Congregation Become a Community That Openly Welcomes People of All Sexual Orientations and Gender Identities* (Washington, DC: National Gay and Lesbian Task Force's Institute for Welcoming Resources, 2013), https://tinyurl.com/y6s6l28y.

3 Matt 10:16.

CHAPTER 5: How Jesus-y Should Our Program Be?

1 He didn't.

CHAPTER 6: What Do LGBTQ Youth Want to Be Called?

1 The terms at the top of the chapter are real, but I'm not going to spend my time defining them. Still, it's worth the energy to research them, learn about the various identities and communities, and be prepared to learn some more new words as you continue your ministry.

2 Brent Pickett, "Homosexuality," *Stanford Encyclopedia of Philosophy*, last modified April 28, 2020, www.plato.stanford.edu/entries/homosexuality.

3 Anna Broadway, "Pink Wasn't Always Girly," *Atlantic*, August 12, 2013, https://tinyurl.com/y4e6tkt2.

4 Ilan H. Meyer, "How Do You Measure the LGBT Population in the U.S.?," Gallup.com, June 27, 2019, https://tinyurl.com/yynd3d3g.

5 Frank Newport, "In U.S., Estimate of LGBT Population Rises to 4.5%," Gallup.com, May, 22, 2018, https://tinyurl.com/y6qcxulq.

6 "Accelerating Acceptance 2017," GLAAD, March 30, 2017, https://tinyurl.com/yxfqzfbj.

7 Brittany Spanos, "Janelle Monáe Frees Herself," *Rolling Stone*, April 26, 2018, https://tinyurl.com/y2kaodob.

CHAPTER 7: What Is the Big Deal about Names?
1 Matt 16:15.

2 "Research Brief: Accepting Adults Reduce Suicide Attempts among LGBTQ Youth," The Trevor Project, June 27, 2019, https://tinyurl.com/y3gg6trf.

CHAPTER 8: How Can the Church Help Youth Wrestle with Identity Questions?
1 Gen 32:28.

2 "Holy Baptism," in *Evangelical Lutheran Worship* (Minneapolis, MN: Augsburg Fortress, 2006), 228.

CHAPTER 9: What Holy Days and Rituals Do LGBTQ Youth Observe? Are These Even Christian?
1 Lily Percy, "Jeanne Manford: A Mother First, Gay Rights Activist Second," *All Things Considered*, NPR, January 12, 2013, https://tinyurl.com/yyd686gm.

2 See appendix B for a list of LGBTQ faith organizations.

CHAPTER 11: When Should We Be Serious and Heavy? When Should We Be Fun and Campy?
1 Vincent Andriani, *Peanut Butter Rhino* (New York: Scholastic, 1995).

CHAPTER 13: When Should I Keep Confidence and When Should I Report?
1 Soon Kyu Choi, Bianca D. M. Wilson, Jama Shelton, and Gary Gates, *Serving Our Youth 2015: The Needs and Experiences of Lesbian, Gay, Bisexual, Transgender, and Questioning Youth Experiencing Homelessness* (Los Angeles: The Palette Fund, True Colors Fund, The Williams Institute, 2015), https://truecolorsunited.org/servingouryouth.

2 Dyana Bagby, "Terrifying Video Shows Violent Altercation after Young Georgia Man Comes Out Gay to Family," *Georgia Voice*, August 28, 2014, https://tinyurl.com/yyzsmwx3.

CHAPTER 15: What Relationship Guidelines Can the Church Teach LGBTQ Youth?
1 Amy Johnson, "Our Whole Lives," United Church of Christ, accessed August 2, 2020, https://tinyurl.com/hdam36c.

CHAPTER 20: How Can We Queer the Youth Ministry Experience?
1 The first part of this chapter is adapted from a workshop that Logan Rimel presented for The Naming Project called "No Purpling: But God Is Purpling All the Time" to teach queer theory as a lens to evaluate youth ministry.

2 This phrase is the inspiration for the title of the popular television show *Queer as Folk*.

3 Cherry Kittredge, "Radclyffe Hall: Queer Christian Themes Mark Banned Book 'Well of Loneliness,'" Q Spirit, August 12, 2019, https://tinyurl.com/yxru7mzx.

4 Marguerite Radclyffe Hall, *The Well of Loneliness* (New York: Anchor Books, 1990), 22.

CHAPTER 21: What about Queering Youth Ministry Songs?

1 Exod 3:13–14.

2 God can't even stay in one tense!

3 Paul Vasile, Music That Makes Community, accessed August 2, 2020, http://www.musicthatmakescommunity.org/.

CHAPTER 22: Does This Mean LGBTQ Youth Might Change My Bible Study?

1 1 Cor 1:18–25.

2 I am glossing over several rather problematic aspects to this story. One is whether the queen was summoned just so the courtiers could gawk at her. Some scholars even suggest she was ordered to appear wearing only a crown. I am also skipping the fact that Esther was likely forced to appear before the king and had little power to refuse.

3 Ruth 1:16.

4 Gen 37:2.

5 Gen 37:3.

6 2 Sam 13:18.

7 Mark 3:34.

CHAPTER 23: What about Working with Other Ministry Organizations That Don't Share My Values about LGBTQ People?

1 You can find a reliable list of prominent anti-LGBTQ advocates along with quotes and references of what exactly they are saying in the Commentator Accountability Project, compiled by GLAAD at www.glaad.org/cap.

2 Maya Rhodan, "Christian Group That Flip-Flopped on Gay Marriage Loses Donors," *Time*, March 28, 2014, https://tinyurl.com/y5f627u7.

3 Jim Beré and Richard Sterns, "World Vision U.S. Board Reverses Decision," World Vision, February 1, 2017, https://tinyurl.com/y6mqgbz5.

CHAPTER 24: What Happens to LGBTQ Youth outside My Youth Group?

1 Hollie Silverman, "Idaho Governor Signs Two Bills That Limit the Rights of Transgender People," CNN, March 31, 2020, https://tinyurl.com/u3bkoy5.

2 "Legislative Tracker: Anti-transgender Legislation Filed for the 2020 Legislative Session," Freedom for All Americans, accessed April 8, 2020, https://tinyurl.com/y25fy728.

CHAPTER 25: Now What?

1 Ps 139.

APPENDIX B: LGBTQ Christian Organizations

1 Meredith Bischoff, "Organizational Partners of IWR," Institute for Welcoming Resources, June 26, 2017, http://www.welcomingresources.org/partners.

2 Jamie Bruesehoff and Lee Zandstra, "Faith, Hope, Love," New Jersey Synod: Evangelical Lutheran Church in America, 2020, http://www.njsynod.org/faith-hope-love.

APPENDIX C: LGBTQ Holy Days for Your Youth Ministry to Commemorate

1 All HIV commemoration day information is taken from www.hiv.gov.

APPENDIX D: Other Helpful Resources

1 "About Believe Out Loud," Believe Out Loud, accessed August 2, 2020, https://tinyurl .com/y5eaavao.

2 Paul Vasile, Music That Makes Community, accessed August 2, 2020, http://www .musicthatmakescommunity.org/.

3 Amy Johnson, "Our Whole Lives," United Church of Christ, accessed August 2, 2020, https://tinyurl.com/hdam36c.